God's Hand at Work

God's Hand at Work

7 True Stories from Africa

To Elizabeth Henderson, with love & best wishes
Joseph Amamoo
Jan. 8. 2015.

Joseph Amamoo

Copyright © 2013 by Joseph Amamoo.

Library of Congress Control Number:		2012923845
ISBN:	Hardcover	978-1-4797-6910-0
	Softcover	978-1-4797-6909-4
	Ebook	978-1-4797-6911-7

All rights reserved. No part of this book may be reproduced or transmitted in any form or by any means, electronic or mechanical, including photocopying, recording, or by any information storage and retrieval system, without permission in writing from the copyright owner.

This book was originally printed in the USA.
UK Edition printed by Tyson Media Group
Published by Joseph Amamoo
Contact Details: Tel: 0208 2006 443
Email: kwaw100@gmail.com
Web: newafricacalls.zoomshare.com or africanreflections.freevar.com

To order additional copies of this book, contact:
Xlibris Corporation
1-888-795-4274
www.Xlibris.com
Orders@Xlibris.com
123771

Contents

Failure And Success 9

A Friend Of Doctors 13

Misfortune, A Blessing In Disguise 31

Musa, Drive Him Out 40

Our Guardian Angel 48

Policia, Please Get Me Out 58

Tropical Down Pour 62

Index 67

I hope and trust that these stories, based on true life experiences, would strengthen all believers' faith in God and also encourage agnostics and atheists that perhaps what they all term or call "coincidence" may have a meaning way beyond their understanding as mortals.

I wish to express my warmest gratitude to Aaron Woods of Ashford, Kent, England, for his invaluable work of typing and checking the manuscript.

Dedicated, with much gratitude to all the Volunteers who have served in Africa and thus contributed enormously to the fight against ignorance, diseases and poverty in Africa, the cradle of Mankind.

Finally, my wife of over fifty years, Breid, has made an enormous contribution to this work in various ways. Indeed, she deserves to be called a coauthor. My gratitude to her is limitless.

Failure And Success

At the age of about eleven, at the end of my elementary school education at the Methodist school at Agona Swedru in Ghana, I sat for the entrance examinations for four secondary schools: Mfantsipim, Adisadel, St. Augustine, and Achimota. To prepare for the tests, I did all the necessary cramming and mock interviews. I tried my best, for I knew too well even at that age that if I did not get any further education, then I was destined to be a failure or, at best, face a very difficult life of relentless labor, hardship, and suffering.

In addition to studying as well as I could, in the few moments that I could snatch from my numerous and laborious home chores, I also prayed hard. For as a firm believer in God and prayers, I felt that my efforts would come to naught if God was not on my side. Again and again, I repeated to myself the famous words of Lord Tennyson, the celebrated British poet: "More things are wrought by prayer than this world dreams of."

Going to Cape Coast for the examinations for the first three institutions was no joke as the fare for both visits was, by local standards, very high. Furthermore, Uncle Fred, my legal guardian and in loco parentis, was not prepared to contribute a penny toward my efforts to get further education. Looking back, I am convinced, without any doubts whatsoever, that they wished that I continued in my status as a virtual slave, if not forever, then at least for a few more years.

With sheer determination and boundless sacrifice, my dear mother came to my rescue. She sold one or two of her jewelry pieces and got me the fares for all the trips by public transport to Cape Coast. The schools were impressive and, to me, daunting. I just could not imagine that I might end up in one of them, God willing! Although poor and hungry, I still had the sense to know that the trials at Cape Coast would be a do-or-die matter for me.

The examination for entrance to Achimota—then British colonial, Africa's equivalent of Eton College in Britain, minus the girls—took place at my school at Agona Swedru, thus not needing any travel from my hometown.

Going over all the questions again and again after the examinations and recalling what I wrote, I could not but conclude that I had done quite well and deserved to be given a chance. After all, I had done all that I could by studying hard and praying hard. What more could I do? Furthermore, I was now out of the cudgels of Uncle Fred and his wife, who had, for five unforgettable years, made my life hell.

About three weeks after the examinations, I went through a lot of sleepless nights awaiting the results with trepidation, for my whole future, like a thin thread, hung on the results. My dear mother was not in the financial position to pay for my secondary education; any offer for a place in any of the schools that did not include a scholarship would be utterly useless to me.

First of the results came from Adisadel College, and it was bad news. I had been rejected outright. I could not understand this hard blow from fate. Why? Next to come was the Roman Catholic institution, St. Augustine's College. More bad news. I was at my wits' end, not knowing what to do other than intensify my prayers. Then out of the blue, there came the good news from the Methodist school Mfantsipim, the alma mater of the internationally famous then UN secretary-general Kofi Annan. Their offer was good, but in reality was of no use to me. For although they had given me a place, the fees were so high, my mother could simply not afford to pay. She and her two sisters, Elizabeth and Dora, were both in tears as I told them in our local language that the offer was in reality a nonstarter.

Beginning to prepare for the worst, I started to draft application letters for a job as a clerk in a local store. Desperation was setting in, and failure was staring me directly in the face.

My reason for worry was because the examination for Achimota College was rather more difficult than those of the other schools. And to complicate matters, the interview was conducted by an Englishman who spoke in an accent that I had never heard before. As I, barefooted and wearing my shabby school uniform of khaki shirt and shorts, stood before him—a tall blond and blue-eyed man with a white shirt and white pair of trousers and smart brown shoes—I was not only terrified but had to strain my ears to follow what he was saying. I smiled broadly to gain sympathy from the white man, for I was dying to go to Achimota to fulfill my boyhood dreams and to also honor my father's hopes and legacy.

My schoolmaster later explained to us students that the white gentleman in question spoke as is done by those who have studied at Oxford or Cambridge University and that they are the people that govern Britain, holding most of the top positions in the civil service, the foreign service, the media, the military, the City of London, the judiciary, the universities, and the field of medicine.

After days of anxiety and emotional torment which appeared to last for months, the results finally came in from the great college one bright Monday morning. As I opened the letter, my hands were trembling as if I was on drugs or seriously ill. The contents were not at all what I expected. For Achimota had given me not only a place but also a scholarship to boot. It was simply incredible. I kept repeating to myself, "God is great. Long may his kingdom come on earth as it is in heaven."

The schools which were in no way in the league of Achimota had rejected me, and the greatest educational institution then in the whole of British colonial Africa had widely opened its arms to me. Why and how did this happen? I put it all down to divine intervention. Come to think of it, I did far better in the examinations at the three schools that rejected me than I did at Achimota.

Momentarily, pulling myself together, I told my mother in our local Fanti language that God had spoken and that I had won a scholarship to the greatest center of educational excellence in Africa. "You must be joking, Joseph," said my dear mother. I repeated the good news loud and clear to my mother and my three aunts. They wept with joy, for by that achievement, I had become the first in my family and indeed the first in the whole town of about twenty thousand people to go to that famous place.

The following Sunday, my mother went to the local Roman Catholic church, of which she was a devoted member, to offer devout prayers of thanks to God. She also made a big contribution to the church to the applause of the whole congregation. However, as a good mother dedicated to the abiding interest and welfare of her eldest son, she was determined to make assurance doubly sure and make certain that no witches or evil eyes torpedoed my future. The day after the church service, she dressed me in white and took me to the local *Juju* man. He was the revered local oculist, herbalist, prophet, seer, and psychotherapist. He was a white-clad bearded man of about fifty years, wearing an array of talismans around his neck and body. My mother gave him two white hens, a white sheep, some money in a white handkerchief, and a bottle of Dutch gin, much favored in Ghana.

The priest smiled broadly while he accepted the presents, repeating to my mother loudly, "You see, I told you so! My powers come from God himself, I assure you."

Even at my tender age, I simply did not believe in his claims and the rituals which were, to me, nothing more than a hodgepodge of autosuggestion, applied with psychology, fear, wishful thinking, and make-believe.

My mother, having paid her dues to God and the *Juju* man, next set about finding the money to buy the clothes and other items required by the school.

The tuck box and its contents all needed money to address. Unfailing in her love and duty to her children, she again sold some of her jewelry. She also dispatched her three sisters to find all the local women in the next two villages who owed her money for clothes and food items that had been sold to them, for some of her creditors appeared to have conveniently forgotten about their debts!

At long last, my mother was able to singlehandedly fulfill all the obligations with minor contributions from her sisters. The days ticked way as I dreamed of what it would be to see that great place that I had heard so much about. Finally, D-day did arrive on a humid Friday morning, three weeks after the arrival of that memorable letter from Achimota. The truck that would take me to Achimota arrived at our house about eight in the morning.

Wearing my smart white shirt and shorts and the college's famous sandals, I climbed on to the truck with pride as my mother and three aunts wept with joy. They were very happy that I was leaving for Achimota but also apprehensive. For no one from the town had ever been to Achimota and returned to tell what life was at the place. It was all hearsay.

The thirty-six-or-so-mile journey took about two hours due to the need for the vehicle to stop a number of times to pick up other passengers. Finally, we arrived at the great place. Without question, it was a fantastic center of educational excellence. The college was a town itself. Spread over thousands of acres, it had its own police station, post office, railway station, zoo, botanical gardens, sports facilities, hospital, water and sewerage system, electric power, and other amenities of modern life. This was at the early part of the twentieth century when such facilities simply did not exist in many towns in Africa.

As no factories or shops were allowed inside, all necessary infrastructures such as these buildings mentioned above had to be built as part of the college. At its peak a quarter of the whole nation's budget for education was spent on Achimota alone.

I consider spending some of the best six years of my life at Achimota a gift from God, and to me, it was only by divine intervention that I got there to begin eating and living as human beings should. The numerous beautiful girls there to look at but not touch were an extra bonus to the glorious life at Achimota.

A Friend of Doctors

From the age of about seven, I always wanted to be a doctor. For I was told by my friends at school that the people with a white coat over their suits and something called a stethoscope around their necks never got sick. And as I did not want to get sick, I felt that it would be an excellent idea to join the band of doctors and also wear the white coat and that nice instrument around my neck.

Furthermore, even at that early age, my dear father had drummed into my head that he wanted me to train as a doctor so that I could help people who were often ill with all types of diseases. So at an early age, I looked forward to that great day when I would, with joy and happiness, join the noble band of doctors, thus becoming a member of the noblest profession in the world, bar the ministry of God.

So at Achimota College, I tried my best to do well at the sciences. I found them exciting, especially biology. But as time went by, it was becoming more and more apparent to all except me that I was not cut out to become a doctor. Still, I persisted, and when the high school leaving examination results came in from Britain, although I had done well in the sciences, I had done even better in English, British history (from the English Revolution, also known as the Glorious Revolution to the Reform Act, 1832), and English literature. I had scored an A (i.e., 70 percent and above) in the two subjects. In English literature, I got a credit (50 to 69 percent), with none of us getting an A in the whole country.

Friends and my English tutors advised me to try and concentrate on the arts as I was better at them effortlessly than in mathematics and the sciences. But I simply refused to heed their advice. So when I started the two-year postsecondary course, I chose science subjects—zoology, botany, physics, and chemistry. As an optional subject, I took current affairs.

I found that grappling with theory in zoology and botany was not too bad, but with the other two subjects, much as I tried to cram as much as I could, I was fighting a losing battle. To compound my problems, I found the practicals a complete nightmare. It was so depressing seeing colleagues sitting on either side of me calmly and neatly dissecting a shark or a rabbit without cutting into major blood vessels. Often in my case, the whole dissection exercise ended with blood spluttered on my glasses and apron. Knowing well that my colleagues were not any more clever than I was and with my secondary school examinations results fresh in my mind, I simply could not understand why I was not making any headway in the science subjects that I had chosen.

Finally, at the end of the two-year course, when the examination results came in from Cambridge University, UK, despite all my stupendous efforts, I had failed in zoology and chemistry but, to my surprise, passed marginally in botany and physics!

Meanwhile, I had a stroke of luck. I applied for a government scholarship program to study medicine in UK. I was called for an interview at Accra and must have done well. For a week or so later, when I telephoned the secretary of the interview committee, he gave me the good news that I was among the six or so successful candidates and that I would be receiving the official letter shortly.

My joy was boundless as I mused over this great news. At long last, it appeared that God had not forsaken me. Day after day, I walked to the local post office in my hometown, Agona Swedru, to check on the arrival of that letter. At that stage in my life, common-sense and a modicum of realism should have taught me that I was on the wrong career path. But nevertheless, I decided to carry on whatever the sacrifice and failures. The letter that I was expecting never arrived. Somehow, my name had disappeared from the list mysteriously. Subsequently, I learnt that some rich "big man" had "done something" to the list, and hence, the elimination of my name.

So after about two years teaching science at a famous secondary school in Kumasi, Ghana's second city, I entered the University of Ghana at Legon to study for a bachelor of science degree in physics, chemistry, and zoology. Again, the same old intractable headache with practicals in zoology, physics and chemistry reared their ugly heads. Indeed, during an experiment in organic chemistry one hot afternoon, I nearly blew up the whole laboratory and myself if it weren't for the timely intervention of the chemistry professor who was supervising the practicals.

After three years of hard slogging and many hours of sleep deprivation, when the results of the examinations came in from London University, I had failed by a few marks. "What on earth was happening?" I asked myself again and again. "Who was it that determinedly was thwarting my efforts to join the noble profession?" Although not in any way superstitious, my thoughts were beginning to revolve on the possibility that some spirit or gods must be conniving together to deprive me of my life ambition.

The thought of letting down myself and my late father filled me with trepidation and much anxiety.

Although I do not believe in so-called witches as they are simply figments of fertile imaginations, my dear mother, who was a strong Roman Catholic, was of the firm conviction that some evil forces were at work against her eldest son. And being the good, devoted mother that she was, she spent a lot of money on *Juju* men and acclaimed prophets and seers to help get rid of the catalogue of bad luck. My advice to her that the so-called prophets and *Juju* men with acclaimed magical powers were practically all rogues and charlatans out to make money for themselves through their invocation of the name of God, left her unmoved in her determination to consult them for my welfare.

Dejected and on the brink of losing faith in God because I simply could not understand why my peers no more intelligent than I were succeeding while I was failing again and again, I sometimes wondered whether God was on my side or if he had abandoned me. In fact, for a short period in my life, I became an atheist. Of course, looking back more maturely, I find that my stance was rather unreasonable and at the height of folly and arrogance. For to argue that there is no God because one was having a series of misfortunes and negative experiences means that there is God only if one is having a chain of success and nice time. It took me sometime to disabuse myself of this puerile and rather naive way of thinking.

Surviving the stinging blows of life yet having vowed to myself and to the spirit of my father that I would be a doctor one day come what may, I resigned from my position as a science teacher at a major secondary boarding school in Cape Coast, Ghana, sold my radiogram, which was my major possession then, and left by sea for the country where other Africans that I knew had gone, studied, and prospered. After all, if they could make it in Britain, why couldn't I?

After a two-week voyage with very little money in my pocket but brimful of enthusiasm and ambition, it was with heavenly delight that I set foot on English soil. My ordeal in a cramped fourth-class cabin in a French boat had ended. The first thing that I did after settling down in London was to resume my pursuit of my medical ambition. For in spite of my earlier setbacks, I possessed the minimum qualifications for entry to a medical school.

Early on a wintry morning in November, shivering but determined, I found my way to a library and sat down. I pulled from the breast pocket of my coat, a copy of a little book titled *So You Want to Be a Doctor*. I perused it again and then wrote by hand ten copies of applications to the medical schools listed at the back of the booklet.

A couple of weeks later, in anticipation of getting into a medical school, I registered at the Regents Polytechnic in London to study biochemistry and physiology. My view was that the course which I was undertaking would help in my medical studies even if I did not complete the degree program.

In a matter of weeks, I received a few replies to my applications. They were mostly negative, but three or four called me for an interview, among them was Manchester University. And it was on my train journey from London to that great city that I saw snow for the first time. The journey was going smoothly, and I was engrossed in a novel by Ian Fleming. Suddenly, on raising my head, I saw something like a large spotlessly white blanket on both sides of me. Momentarily, I was taken aback then I quickly pulled myself together and said, "Ah, this is snow!" I smiled to myself as my eyes were glued to the snow. This was something that I had studied about in my geography classes for my secondary school in Cambridge certificate examinations but had never seen in my whole life. It looked very white and just as described in the geography text books.

Happily, the interview went rather well, and a few days later, I received an offer that I was on the waiting list. In the course of time, I got similar offers from three other medical schools. However, waiting for months without any firm offer, I began to feel frustrated and depressed. I felt that once again, God had let me down. My feelings of disappointment were heightened when off and on I came across Ghanaian friends of mine in Britain who were happily pursuing their medical studies. I felt deeply that I had been a failure and also let down my father.

One afternoon, while walking from Temple Tube station in London toward Fleet Street, I noticed a large building called Middle Temple. I knew that it was one of the law schools in London. Walking in, I introduced myself to the elderly white gentleman on duty at the reception. Politely, I asked him the requirements to register as a student. From what he told me, I had more than the minimum requirements needed. So there and then, I filled the relevant form and issued a check for the required fee of three hundred pounds (about six hundred US dollars then). And that is how the pursuit of my ambition to become a doctor ended, and my profession as a barrister began. I felt that I had done everything humanly possible to join the great and noble profession but that for one reason or another, my ambition could not be fulfilled. Fate appeared set against me

My great respect and admiration for doctors dates from the day that I lost the battle to join them. They had succeeded where I had failed. But in the process, I had acquired enough knowledge in medicine to be able to read medical reports and articles and talk intelligently with doctors about my own health problems and those of my family. Furthermore, later in life, I was practicing as a lawyer; my modest knowledge of medicine came in very handy when dealing with criminal cases and issues involving disputed paternity, deaths, and in suspicious circumstances. Often I felt that I had an unfair advantage over my lawyer friends on the other side that had no brush with science, let alone with anatomy or physiology.

Having closed the chapter on my aborted medical ambition, I set about with my law studies, working also as a journalist and later as a diplomat. Eight years after giving up on medicine, I had become the editor of the Ghanaian Times. It was then the most influential daily newspaper in Ghana. The country's equivalent to America's *Washington Post* and Britain's the *Times*.

At the end of my spell as editor, I resigned to enter politics. The choice before me was to join either the Progress Party, a center-right party which had been in opposition to the defunct Nkrumah regime and whose ambassador I had been before being sacked, or join the old Nkrumah party, disgraced, split asunder, and reorganized under a new name called the National Alliance of Liberals. Its national leader was an outstanding man who, after faithfully serving Nkrumah as his deputy and later as finance minister (secretary of the treasury), had spoken against Nkrumah's growing dictatorship and was listed for arrest and detention without trial. Fortunately for him, on a tipoff from a member of the feared security service, he managed to flee the country and stayed in exile till the overthrow of Nkrumah.

Due to my mother's wealth, reputation, and influence in our hometown called Agona Swedru, I knew for sure that I would win election to Parliament (Congress) on whichever political party ticket that I ran. Indeed, the *Washington Post* correspondent covering the elections had in an article after visiting Agona Swedru, dubbed my mother as "The Rose Kennedy of Agona Swedru." She was such a great and powerful force for good in the town itself and in the surrounding towns and villages.

So after much heart searching and numerous discussions with my unpaid advisor, confidant, psychologist, and public relations guru, doubling also as the family matriarch, I decided to join the center-right party, following firm invitations from the leaders of both political parties.

With my past experience in election campaigns in London and being a keen student of election campaigns and strategies in both the United States of America and the United Kingdom and as my opponents did not have in any way the funds and vehicles at my disposal, I won easily, getting just over 70 percent of the votes cast. In a five-race contest, I think that I did not do badly, considering that I had not lived in the town for several years.

Straightaway after my election victory was announced to deafening public applause, I drove to the capital city, Accra. From there, I telephoned my wife with the good news. For much against her will, I had persuaded her to leave for London with our two babies as I knew that the campaign was going to be rather rough and enervating in a country without a comprehensive network of smooth roads and railway system. So after her participation in the launch of the campaign at a mass public rally in my hometown at which her blonde hair and beauty had caused much excitement and approval, especially among the women, she left for London protesting to the last minute.

For the next few days, I waited patiently for the telephone to ring with good news. Already before and during the elections, there were rumors that if my party won, I might be appointed as a minister or deputy minister in the ministry of foreign affairs or education or information; either of these would have fitted my background perfectly.

But I was not in the position to, in any way, influence the appointments. I was urged by friends and supporters to call at the residence of the victorious party leader, ostensibly to congratulate him as others were known to be doing. However, I felt it morally repugnant to call on him to lobby for a job under the pretext of going to congratulate him on his landslide victory. Readers may care to note that under the system of government that we were practicing in Ghana under our new constitution, one had to be a member of Parliament or Congress before appointment in the government or administration as opposed to the system in the United States, where under their constitution, you cannot be in Congress and at the same time be in the executive department or administration.

Also, as I was the ambassador of Nkrumah, although I was dismissed before his overthrow, my connection with our party leader was not as strong as those who had been allies of his for many years. As such when the time for the appointments came, I had no choice but to wait, watch, and pray. This is precisely what I did till a few days after our victory. My telephone rang one Saturday night. It was a call from the Reuters correspondent in Accra. He wanted information from me about the newly appointed foreign minister. At the end of our brief chat, he asked me whether I knew that the new government or administration had been announced. When I told him that I did not, he kindly read out the list to me in a slow, calm voice. First was the cabinet, and my name was not on it. Then he began to read out the list of the deputy ministers or secretaries. Again, my name was nowhere until at the very end, he called my name. I nearly did not make it, although my election victory in percentage terms was among the highest in the country. Additionally, the party leader who was to be appointed the prime minister (leader of government) had personally told me that the rally which I organized in my hometown that he addressed at the penultimate phase of the campaign, was the biggest in the whole nation, apart from the one in Kumasi, Ghana's second city.

A few days after the announcement of the government (administration), we were sworn in at the Castle (Ghana's White House) by the prime minister, in the presence of specially invited guests including our loved ones. Needless to state, my dear wife was there to share in the day of glory. After the event, it began to dawn on me that all the disappointments with my failure to become a doctor indeed had a purpose. It appeared as if there was a rhyme and reason behind all the past frustrations and chain of ill luck. I was destined not to be a doctor but to be an overall supervisor and political boss of doctors!

Throwing myself in my new job with the dedication of a born again Christian and the energy of a young marathon runner, I set out to establish at the Ministry of Health, that I had a divine mission to accomplish. My grand strategy was to pay unscheduled visits to hospitals. Those that I found to be not working as they should or collecting their pay for doing little or nothing or stealing medicines or the food of patients were given a robust verbal lashing. In a few instances, they were suspended on the spot, with further disciplinary action to follow. I felt that in a poor developing country, those who were trusted to look after the sick, poor, and needy had no moral right whatsoever to tamper with public funds or property for their benefit.

As such, at every opportunity, I made it my mission to castigate and shame those caught wrongdoing. Frequently, I told my impromptu audiences that while professional wrongdoing by medical or health personnel in developed countries was bad and serious enough, such activities in a developing country such as Ghana, where sadly, many of the people are illiterate or ignorant or helpless, were absolutely immoral, obscene, and grossly criminal as the victims were invariably poor and helpless. Naturally, the more I carried on with my evangelical crusade, the greater became my unpopularity. But as I felt that I had been placed in that position by God through the prime minister for a noble purpose, I did not worry unduly about my plummeting popularity. After all, I was not engaged in a beauty contest.

The joys and sorrows that I had during my period at the ministry of health are too many to narrate here. They all fit into the grand program that I felt was devised by an unseen hand, which to me was the hand of God. The skeptic or atheist may think that I am rather naive and simpleminded. And in a democratic society, they are fully entitled to their views. And like Voltaire, the celebrated French writer and philosopher, although I disagree with their opinions, I would defend to the death their right to express them.

Of all the numerous incidents during my stewardship at the department of health, three in particular stand out vividly in my mind. The first involved grappling with a longstanding official red tape and culture that had caused and continued to cause many civil servants and their families immense, easily avoidable misery and hardship. One wet afternoon, after an excellent kosher lunch with my wife, I went to my office in a rather happy mood. As soon as I sat down, my secretary came to inform me that a young army captain would like to see me for a few minutes as he had an urgent problem. Reluctantly, I agreed to his request although he did not have an appointment with me. Next, a young officer walked in who saluted smartly and sat down at my request. "Sir, I am very sorry to bother you, but I have a major distressing problem, Mr. Minister. In fact, you taught me chemistry and biology at Premco a few years ago."

"Good, nice to hear this, and how can I help or assist you, Captain?"

"Sir, about four months ago, my wife, who is a nurse at Tarkwa, was transferred to Accra and up till now, she has not been paid."

"Why?" I interjected.

"Sir, anytime we inquire at the accounts office, we are told that the LPC has not yet come from her last station. Mr. Minister, we are in dire financial straits. We need help from God acting through you."

I listened calmly then asked, "Forgive my ignorance, captain. But what is LPC?"

"Sir, it is the certificate stating the last pay and date at the station before the transfer."

"I see, and without that, your wife cannot be paid? Good Lord, four months without pay. This is absolute nonsense!"

"Yes, sir."

"Don't worry, Captain, I will resolve everything in a couple of days or so. You leave it in my hands and call me the day after tomorrow in the afternoon, around three. I am very sorry to hear of what you and your wife have gone through, but take it from me, she will get her pay at the end of this month. Only two more weeks to wait, and it will all be over. Warmest regards to your wife. Goodbye and see you soon. By the way, I hope that you have not forgotten all the chemistry and biology that I taught you."

"No, sir." We both smiled as he mentioned amoeba and the benzene cycle. He saluted, bowed, and left as a happy man.

As soon as he left, I called in the accounts officer and told him of the predicament of the captain's wife, the nurse recently transferred from Tarkwa to Accra. With a straight face, he told me that he knew about the case. So I instructed him to get her file and rectify the position by giving the nurse at least three months' pay, and the figures reconciled when the LPC reached him.

He agreed with me that was the best course of action to avoid further misery and suffering to the nurse and her family. He left with clear instructions to bring the file to me himself the following day. And he left in an amiable disposition. The next day, he came to me with a long cock-and-bull story that he had searched everywhere but could not find the file. I asked him to try again and report with the good news in the evening before closing. He dutifully reported as agreed but with the same negative report that the file of the stranded nurse could not be traced.

So trying to control my anger, I asked him, "Did you get your salary last month?"

"Yes, sir," he quickly replied.

Then I continued, "If you are unable to locate the file and reconcile the figures as we agreed, then simple—at the end of this month, I will see to it that you do not—I repeat—do not get your salary. And you would then get a little taste of what it is to be without a salary for even a month, let alone four solid months."

He stood speechless and appeared shocked. "Have I made myself absolutely clear?"

"Yes, sir."

"You may go now. See you tomorrow. Thank you," I concluded.

My anger was generated by my firm conviction that the chap knew all the time where the file was but was refusing to do his duty until and unless the nurse or her husband did something. Otherwise, the file which had disappeared into thin air or lost its legs could not be found or could not move to its proper destination. It appeared that some of the personnel at the health ministry had not paid even a tiny hoot to all my frequent exhortations on accountability by public officers and their moral and professional duty and obligation to do that for which they were paid by the taxpayers. I was distressed by the sheer callousness and crass inhumanity of some human beings to other human beings.

As I reflected on the grossly unprofessional behavior of the public servant, I decided that the best way to teach him a good lesson, even if he miraculously found the file, was to suspend his pay for at least a month for wasting my time, the government's time, and the needless aggravation and distress that he had wittingly caused the army officer and his hapless wife. Also, I felt that my contemplated disciplinary action would send a strong message—crystal clear and unambiguous—to his colleagues that I was indeed determined to rid of the system of corruption and utterly unacceptable behavior and action from the people who were duty bound, moral considerations apart, to serve diligently those who were at immense personal sacrifice paying their wages and salaries.

The following morning after my threat of salary suspension, my friend came in full of smiles, with the file in his hand. According to him, after much search, he had found the file hidden in another file, beneath a big file beside a green file under a yellow file."

I smiled as he went on then suddenly cut him short. "Please stop. Do you take me for a fool?" I asked.

"No, sir," he responded quickly.

"Then why tell me this long yarn about the miraculous discovery of the file when you knew all along where it was? In fact, I venture to add that it was in your top drawer all the time, and you were waiting for the nurse or her husband to do something before the file would move. Do you forget that I am a Ghanaian like you and that I am aware of many of the dirty tricks that some public servants resort to when dealing with the public who pay their salaries?"

He stood there speechless and Sphinx-like. I went on. "By the way, have you prepared the check for three months' pay as I instructed?"

"Yes, Mr. Minister," he replied as he opened the "long lost and found file."

My friend then gave me a brown official envelope addressed to the nurse, care of Capt. Kofi Wright. Fifth Battalion, Ghana Army, Burma Camp, Accra.

He politely gave me the letter, bowed, and said, "Sir, I am very sorry for what I did."

"That's all right and thank you very much. I hope that we are now friends again. You may go now," I concluded. But when he was near the exit door, I said, "Ah! I forgot one thing, do come in."

He stood again before me and then heard in his unbelieving ears. "One, you have done a lot of damage to an innocent nurse and her family. Two, you have fallen on your duty as a public servant of the republic. Three, you have wasted my time and treated me like a fool. Four, you have wasted a lot of government time and therefore money. Five, by your inaction on this matter, you have played into the hands of white racists who are always delighted to gather evidence of wrongdoing by black people to justify their obnoxious, unscientific, and baseless theories and views. In other words, by your gross dereliction of your duty, you have let down not only the nation, but also the black race. What you did was absolutely disgraceful coming from a senior official of your caliber. I understand that you have a wife and five children. Otherwise, I would recommend your immediate suspension for four months without pay."

I paused as he looked at me intently. "Well, in the circumstances, only a month's salary will be deducted." He stared at me as if hit directly by a low-grade bomb. He was pleading incoherently, asking to be forgiven. Suddenly, he held my foot in the traditional way of requesting forgiveness.

"Please get up, for I am not God. Only before Him do we kneel." He stood up and resumed his litany of apologies and expressions of remorse. I smiled at him, then said, "Well, you leave me no choice but to relent. But please, never do this dastardly thing again. Furthermore, I am letting you off scot-free on condition that you embark on an evangelical crusade among your colleagues and friends that they never behave as you did and always treat members of the public, their paymasters, as they would like to be treated themselves. Agreed?"

"Yes, sir, and thank you very much, Mr. Minister. May God bless you and your family."

"And yours too, goodbye."

The following day, the captain called at my office and collected the check; he left a very happy man. However, this little episode drew my attention to the misery and suffering of many public service personnel who were in similar situations as the nurse but did not know any person in high authority or have a husband with some connections among the high and mighty, and thus, have to suffer in silence for long periods.

As I reflected on their plight, I got in perspective why again and again I was stopped from becoming a doctor so that I could end being a friend and supervisor of doctors attending to their problems about salaries, working conditions, promotions, and transfers, adjudicating disputes among them and contributing to the improvement of the quality of life of people through my services to the ministry of health,

The second memorable episode worth narrating concerned a new mobile dental clinic. During an official visit to a provincial hospital not far from the capital city, a few months into my work, I heartily congratulated the staff at the hospital for the high standard of cleanliness of the whole place. Of particular interest to me were the kitchen and the toilets, which are major sources of infection.

I had nothing but fulsome praise for the good work done by the hospital personnel, considering the challenging circumstances and conditions under which they worked.

Toward the end of the visit, I was being taken to see a new annex building, a maternity ward, when I noticed a new vehicle parked under some bushes and trees. Inquiring about the vehicle, I was told by the chief administrator that it was a new vehicle that needed servicing. I found it odd that a new vehicle should need servicing, so I asked more questions and insisted that I should be taken to have a look at the vehicle.

"Mr. Minister, you have other engagements and time is running fast," said the chief administrator. I smelled a rat when I saw him wink to his deputy, a pretty woman of about forty, who—I had learnt only recently—joined the hospital after many years of studying and working in the United States of America.

Feeling rather uncomfortable about what was happening, I decided against the protestations of the administrator and some of his colleagues accompanying me to walk to the vehicle. We had to navigate some muddy patches before reaching the vehicle. And what I saw was mindboggling. An almost new, mobile, dental clinic, stuck in the mud for two months.

"Why, what is happening?" I asked

The chief administrator was the first to speak. "Sir, we have tried to get spare parts for the vehicle since it broke down, but there has been no response from Accra."

"What? How long has this vehicle been stuck here in the mud?" I asked again as I noticed many termites, cockroaches, flies and their families competing with each other to enter the vehicle.

"Two months, sir," he said.

"This is a sheer waste of valuable national assets. While the vehicle stands here deteriorating, thousands of our villagers have to do without urgently needed dental care and treatment."

I was boiling inside as I spoke. Equally irritated and annoyed without measure were my listeners who were not at all used to such forthright talk from a government minister.

I continued, "This vehicle, I learned, was donated by one of our donor-partners."

"Germany, sir," one of the officers said loudly.

"And here we are, not putting it to the proper use for which it was meant. The taxpayers of these countries send us vehicles such as this one at considerable expense and sacrifice, and the least that we can do or is expected of us is to look after them properly and use them to serve the poor and the needy in the rural areas. What is simpler and easier than this?"

They continued to listen to me in utter silence as I went on with my monologue.

"As you all know, my visit ends tomorrow evening. I expect to see this vehicle seen to, fixed, extricated from the mud, and running before I leave, or I am afraid, some heads will roll. I mean it, some heads will roll!"

We walked back to the main building in complete silence. From there, I inspected a female ward, where the conditions were not at all bad. It smelled of fresh paint as it had been recently refurbished with a grant from the USAID —United States Agency for International Development.

My farewell dinner that night was a rather subdued, formal affair. For by then, the hospital staff had become fed up with my presence. But they did their level best not to show their inner feelings. The beaming smiles on their faces were exactly opposite to their inner feelings, I speculated.

Noticing three white women among the guests, I asked who they were. And I was told that two were Peace Corps volunteers from the United States of America, and the other was from Germany, also a volunteer.

Knowing that these three women and others like them happily left their nice and beautiful homes in developed countries to work for free in parts of Ghana that many local medical or health personnel flatly refused to be posted it made me reflect for a few minutes on black and white relations on the global field.

After the dinner, I listened with a wry smile on my face as the chief nurse gave the vote of thanks. It was full of flattering comments on my sagacity and dedication to the national cause, love of humanity, and the plight of the common man.

Instinctively, I felt that she did not believe a word of what she was saying. So as I listened, I had great difficulty in stopping myself from spurting out, "Tell it to the Marines."

The dinner ended on a happy note. At the informal tête-à-tête with the guests before they left, I called in the three volunteers and congratulated and thanked them for their noble services to the poor and suffering in Africa.

My visit ended happily. Just after lunch, with about four hours to go before my return to the capital city, the chief administrator came to tell me that two experienced mechanics from the head office in Accra had brought with them the necessary spare parts and had repaired the vehicle to running condition.

"True?" I asked in utter disbelief.

"Yes, Mr. Minister," he proudly responded.

"Good, let's go and have a look."

So, accompanying him and three others, we went to the vehicle. It was now cleaned up and dressed like a bride on her wedding day. The mud and filth had all disappeared, so had the termites, cockroaches, flies, and their families. I was ushered into the vehicle, which was in a tiptop condition. Spontaneously, we all clapped briefly as I was driven for a few minutes around the hospital.

I got out of the vehicle, congratulated the chief administrator and his staff, and concluded with the words, "The next important challenge is that this expensive, new mobile dental clinic goes to the remote villages to attend to the care and treatment of the people. They have waited long enough."

The chief administrator quickly said, "Yes, sir. Sure!"

"Good, very good, I expect a full report in two weeks, please, don't forget." With that, my brief but memorable tour came to an end, I am sure to the great relief of all the hospital staff.

The third incident at the health ministry had some international ramifications, for during the presidency of Ghana's founding father, Dr. Kwame Nkrumah, the Eastern communist countries were very popular in Ghana, especially as the president geared up his anticolonialist, anticapitalist, antiracism program.

Indeed, these countries were courted not only for funds, but also for educational opportunities and facilities, for during the British colonial period, students who wanted to further their education had only British universities to resort to. Thus, in the field of medical care, the colonial government awarded annually five or six scholarships for deserving students to study medicine in Britain. In a population of about five million then and with only around five hundred doctors in the country, the number of government scholarships was grossly inadequate. For this figure worked out to around one doctor for ten thousand potential patients. Even with the input of foreign doctors as volunteers or missionaries, the position was dire and unacceptable.

So as soon as he became Ghana's leader, Nkrumah, in a response to the public outcry and incessant demand for more doctors, set up the scholarship secretariat in Accra. And through it, got hundreds of scholarships for Ghanaian students to go to the Eastern European countries and study, particularly medicine. In view of the fact that in many remote areas, a doctor was a rare species and a visit was a major celebratory event, Nkrumah's policy made perfect sense. But his critics expressed the fear that some of the doctors might return home indoctrinated with the ideology of communism. This was anathema in a country where about 70 percent were Christians or claimed to be so, with 15 percent Muslims and the rest being atheists, agnostics, and followers of traditional African faiths.

With English as their official language, the students had to grapple with the language of instruction in Hungary, the Soviet Union, or other communist state as they found themselves. Additionally, they had the harsh winters in Central Europe to cope with. But they were happy to bear and grin through all the hurdles and hardships before them as they were rather fortunate to get the chance to educate themselves and acquire a profession whose members are treated almost like gods in their country of birth.

By the irony of fate, by the time the first batch of the doctors trained in Russia and the Eastern Bloc began to return home, the administration of Nkrumah had been overthrown in a military coup. And all ideas pro-Nkrumah or any procommunist or socialist, were considered and treated at best suspicious or at worst downright dangerous and to be avoided like the plague. "Russian doctors," as the media enthusiastically called the newly arrived doctors, became the victims of the campaign to root out all things, persons, and ideas that looked socialist or pro-Russian.

Into this boiling cauldron of anti-Russian sentiment flew in the first batch of Russian trained doctors. They spoke Russian, had qualified as doctors in Russia, and were ready and willing to serve their country. But the cold war was at its apogee. Also, all the members of the medical establishment were from renowned British medical schools. They were proud of their firm connections in Britain. They were of the firm conviction that the newly arrived doctors were unfit to practice medicine, except after a minimum period of retraining.

Some hawks among them wanted a complete retraining program for the hapless young doctors. The debate on the fate of the doctors spilled from the hallowed precincts of academic medicine into the public arena. And the media generally joined in bashing the "Russian doctors."

Despite the glaring need for doctors, the new military junta chased out the Russian doctors, lock, stock, and barrel.

As it was the job of the Ministry of Health to recruit and employ doctors and finding the cost of recruiting foreign doctors from Britain was very expensive, the issue of the Russian trained doctors became of much concern to the ministry. For if the only medical school in the land and the medical registration authorities would not register the doctors, then there was no way that the government could employ them. Nor could they practice privately on their own.

The debate over this issue dragged on and became so intense that some of the doctors left the country out of frustration and anger. They went to neighboring African countries where they were welcomed with open arms. Some of them stayed and bore the humiliation and public ridicule, for they were determined to stay and serve their people whatever the distress and embarrassment that they had to bear.

At the Ministry of Health head office in Accra, the minister, the chief director, and I had a number of meetings to resolve the issue. The medical establishment was represented by the dean of the medical school, the head of human resources, and the director of studies. The government side included the minister of health, the chief director (chief of staff), and me.

Each meeting ended in a stalemate. The dean and his colleagues were absolutely convinced that it would be a disaster and against the public good for the Russian doctors as they were dubbed to be allowed to practice without further and rigorous retraining, at least for a couple of years or so. Armed with impressive figures, the syllabus of their school (which was affiliated to London University), and their program of teaching, they vividly contrasted these with what they said were their Russian counterpart.

Both the minister and the chief director were not doctors. And although I had a good idea what being a doctor entailed, namely the long, relentless hours of study, the intricacies of that mindboggling subject in biochemistry called

Krebs cycle, I was in no way a doctor. So none of us three were in a strong position to challenge the eminent dean, the first African to train as a surgeon in the United Kingdom.

One fine afternoon, fortified with a good kosher lunch with my dear wife, I went to yet another scheduled meeting. Luckily for me, the minister, who by virtue of his position and rank was to chair the meeting, was away on an important national assignment. So the honor of chairing the meeting fell on me. I was determined to end this endless series of meetings, always terminating in a draw.

Therefore, after the venerable dean had rehashed his case in the best Queen's English, I respectfully requested a brief break for a private individual reflection, for emotions were starting to rise. During the break, I wondered how it was that the country that had recently put the first satellite in space, followed by the first human being in space, orbiting round the world, could not produce good doctors.

If as the Russian embassy in Accra and the doctors themselves asserted, the African students and the Russian local students were trained by the same teachers in the same classrooms and laboratories, dissecting the same cadavers, using the same textbooks, and sitting and passing the same examinations, then it was difficult to rationalize why the hapless African doctors were inferior to their counterparts trained in Britain or elsewhere.

Furthermore, I recalled that one of the fundamental structures of modern chemistry, the Periodic Table, was devised by a Russian named Mendeleev. Much of the foundation work on superconductivity and supercold temperatures was done by Dr. Peter Kapitza, a Russian physicist. Among the major pioneers in the use of plastics as artificial organs or tissues was a Russian surgeon. It was a Russian doctor and physiologist, by the name of Pavlov, who started the work that has become one of the pillars of modern neurosurgery.

Although space science is not directly related to medicine, in the heat of the debate, one could not but recall that the first living or nonliving things, including the first human being to orbit the earth were put there by Russian science.

The more I reflected on some of the undisputed scientific and medical achievements of Russians, I could not but conclude that the whole saga that surrounded the Russian doctors was motivated by gross prejudice, fuelled by professional and political animus. Even if one concedes that British medicine was more advanced than that in the Eastern Communist Bloc, to have insisted on a full retraining program for the doctors would have been grossly unfair to them.

Admittedly, at the height of the public's and media's negative reaction to the doctors, there were all sorts of fanciful rumors about their incompetence and low professional standards. For example, I was told that one of them, in an operation to remove an inflamed appendix, had perforated the uterus (womb) with fatal and distressing consequences. This story, whether true or false, added to the growing resentment against the beleaguered doctors. Rapidly, the whole debate had degenerated from anticommunism into unnecessary anti-Russian campaign, with even some educated people not prepared to draw the line between the two.

My training as a lawyer and as a scientist (although I marginally failed the degree, thanks to the invisible British examiners!) had taught me to study the facts before me and draw reasonable and fair conclusions from them, keeping my own emotions and feelings firmly under control. As such, when the meeting resumed and we started to rehash our positions, I respectfully suggested that as a compromise, the Russian doctors be allowed to register and placed temporarily under supervision, working under more experienced physicians and surgeons.

I knew from my experience in Britain, Ghana, Hungary, and Austria that often in many major government decisions, "temporary" has a knack of maturing into "permanent."

I watched the dean as he held a tête-à-tête talk with one of his colleagues. I kept my fingers crossed, hoping for the best. Then suddenly, to my surprise, he said, "Well, Mr. Minister, in the circumstances, we accept your suggestion, and thank you very much on my own behalf and on behalf of my colleagues here present." Thus, ended the torment and ordeal of the Russian doctors, saved by one who failed to become a doctor but ended as a friend and supervisor of doctors. In a matter of a few weeks, the Russian doctors' episode had disappeared from the psyche and radar of the media and the public.

Lo and behold, while I was in prison, one of the doctors that I had never met, hearing of my predicament, drove all the way from upcountry to Accra with his Russian wife who was a dentist and sought my wife and children. Finding them after much difficulty, they gave them a lot of fresh food and some money. At a time when family and friends had vamoosed into thin air, and the bank accounts, properties, and other assets of my wife and me had been frozen by the military junta, the gifts to my wife and children were like gold and silver.

Furthermore, on my release, following fifteen months of hardship and "enforced sabbatical leave," this generous and nice couple were among the first to call at my home to welcome me back. They brought even more food and money. This was the first time that I had met them and it was a pleasant and a memorable experience.

Yes, as in all instances of doing good, not only the beneficiary but the doer also benefits from his good deeds, albeit indirectly. For when placed by destiny in a position to help my fellow citizens, I did my duty and the right thing by helping the sick, the ailing and dying, and the needy through helping the Russian doctors. It never crossed my mind for a moment that in a matter of two years, I would be benefitting enormously from my own actions.

Misfortune, A Blessing In Disguise

I am sure all readers have had the experience at one time or another when a major incident or event looked upon as a disaster or misfortune, without rhyme or reason, later turned out to be a major blessing of immense benefits. Well, this story is a case in point. While the Ghana ambassador in Hungary and to the International Atomic Energy Agency in Vienna, Austria, I had read and heard disturbing reports about the growing trends toward dictatorship in Ghana by the founder of the republic, President Kwame Nkrumah. Disturbed and uneasy that I was about these reports, I tried to salve my conscience by saying to myself frequently that maybe, as a developing country, Ghana needed a strong leader to drag the nation by the scruff of its neck, screaming and screeching, to the status of a semi-developed country. And that to achieve this goal, a measure of strong arm actions are necessary and unavoidable. However, as time moved on, I became more and more disturbed with the growing numbers of arrests that were going on in Ghana, and the fact that with alacrity, the great liberator of the country from British colonialism was building, step by step, a civilian dictatorship that was a mockery of the noble ideas of freedom, democracy, and justice that President Nkrumah himself had fervently espoused during the struggle for independence. The great democrat was metamorphosing into a great and ruthless dictator.

Many a time, I agonized, either alone or with my wife, Breid, what was the best thing to do. I did indeed like and admire the president enormously, but he was set on a path that became less and less appealing to me and filled me with growing anger and frustration.

Like millions of people all over the world who are caught in jobs that they need but are revolted by major aspects of their work, I had to consider and balance the needs of my family and myself and the requirements and promptings of my own conscience.

My agonizing was made worst when I was recalled to Ghana as a special aide in the president's office in Accra. What I then saw and heard in whispers from trusted friends and relatives were even more shocking than what I had known while abroad.

So although I went through the motions of doing my work, my soul was long out of the work. With my wife new to the country, I simply did not wish to place her in any position of unnecessary hardship or difficulty, for she had sacrificed an immense lot in marrying me. Giving up her eight-staff strong restaurant business in South London and her two houses liberally filled with antiques, must not have been an easy decision. Even her much-loved dog, a Rottweiler, Bobby, had to be part of the sacrifice that she made for me

So after numerous discussions with her, with the arguments for and against resigning being equally and finely balanced, I decided to carry on.

The continued state of stress that I was in must have led to my developing an obscure autoimmune illness of unknown etiology. I had swollen feet, heavy night sweat, and a persistent cough that would not go away. A series of tests and examinations at the military hospital in Accra, one of the best in West Africa, failed to settle what the cause of my persistent symptoms was. A leading Russian doctor and the chief physician at the hospital, among others, failed to find the cause of my illness. So I was flown to London for treatment by the celebrated English physician, Dr. John Batten, who then was the chief physician at the St. George's Hospital in Hyde Park in London. He had been recommended to my wife and me by the only doctor in Ghana, by the name of Dr. Sammy Brew-Graves, who was able to conclude that from my symptoms, the illness must be sarcoidosis. This US-educated physician, an old Achimotan had hit the nail on the head, medically speaking.

Dr. John Batten, who later became a knight of the realm and chief physician of Her Majesty, the Queen, was at that time, one of the few doctors in the world with a knowledge of this intractable disease. For several months, I was under the care of this outstanding and great man. I had immense and utter confidence in him and that must have contributed to my steady recovery without any treatment whatsoever. I had somehow appeared to have defeated a disease which at that time was suspected of being a cross between cancer and tuberculosis and of greater incidence among black people than white people. It had no known cause and no known cure.

While recuperating from my illness, for an unknown reason, my salary as an ambassador on medical leave was suddenly terminated without any notification or letter. As my wife and I anguished on our predicament, we concluded that my dismissal could not have been caused by the fact that I had been on sick leave for just over a year. After all, there were two or three colleagues of mine in similar situations and for longer periods whose salaries had not been stopped. So we concluded that there must be other reasons. It was then I told my wife that a couple of weeks or so before I had confided in a close relative high in the government, my utter disillusionment and disgust with the continuing trends toward dictatorship, arbitrary rule, and the cult of the personality. I strongly suspect that the gentleman, to whom I had bared my soul and spoken in strict confidence, must have betrayed me in order to protect himself. Now the whole picture became as clear as crystal.

I was frostily received by the head of chancery at the Ghana embassy in London when I called his office to demand an explanation for what had happened to me. The diplomat's attitude to me was neither positive nor negative. It was just blank. I certainly was not shown the usual courtesies as an ambassador, albeit without a station, for I still retained my rank and title well until the misfortune.

Devoid of my salary, I had to fall back on my savings and resort to ad hoc public lectures on Africa, radio and television discussions on Africa, and book reviews. It was apparent that I had not inherited my father's remarkable business acumen. Breid and I, being firm believers in not requesting or taking state welfare benefits and handouts, decided to carry on till the arrival of better days.

On at least two or three occasions, I was tempted to petition the president about the termination of my appointment and salary. But again and again, my inner still voice kept telling me, "Joseph. Don't, don't. Soldier on." With a wife and two babies to look after and an Irish nanny to pay, life was not at all easy.

So indeed, we carried on as best as we could. Suddenly, on a bright wintry morning at about six o'clock, our telephone rang continuously. The date was February 24, 1966. It was a day that I cannot ever forget. The caller was a brother of one of the government ministers that I knew well. His news was that the BBC World Service had just announced that there had been a military coup in Ghana and that the government had been overthrown, Parliament dissolved, the sole party abolished, its assets confiscated to the state, and all government ministers and top party officials arrested and detained. Some, according to his story, had been beaten or at least molested. And a government minister who was trying to flee, dressed as a heavily pregnant woman had been ceased at the Ghana-Togo border, roughed up and beaten by the soldiers.

A couple of hours later, he called again to tell me that he had heard from Ghana that many ambassadors and high profile senior party officials and some civil servants had also been arrested, and that all the editors of the state-owned newspapers and the state radio had been arrested and given a very pleasant treatment before being shoved into prison. Both calls of his left me completely speechless, and although Breid, with her usual exuberance for life, tried to bring normality to our home, I simply could not pull myself together for the import of the news to sink in properly.

In rapid succession, the new military junta announced the seizure by military decrees of all the assets of the arrested people and their wives and traceable mistresses. Overnight, the great and mighty had fallen from grace to grass. The harrowing situation filled me with much despair. I was really sad for them, particularly so for my former diplomat colleagues and journalists, who unfortunately for them, had been at the helm when disaster struck. The whole wheel of fortune had turned full circle. All those who, in one way or another, had been victimized by the defunct regime or had lost their jobs or positions or had left the country to avoid arrest had become national heroes.

The next couple of days brought a litany of bad news. Four prominent ambassadors had been arrested and molested before detention. Some of the ex-ministers had been physically assaulted. A well-known judge had been sacked with his boss, the chief justice, and both thrown into prison. As I knew well many of those in trouble, I was very sorry for them.

For me, the coup suddenly led to a number of telephone calls from some of my Ghanaian friends and others, asking whether I would be going back to serve the new regime. My wife and I followed with great interest, the unfolding events in Ghana as reported on the BBC and independent television channels.

About six months after the military coup, I received a telephone call one morning, at around ten-thirty, from the head of Chancery. It was the same gentleman that a few months earlier had given me a rather unfriendly welcome when I called on him at his office. Surprisingly, he sounded very friendly and over courteous in his tone, repeating frequently, "Your Excellency," as the conversation proceeded. He told me that he had just received a telex message from the Castle in Accra (Ghana's White House) instructing him to ask me whether I would accept to become an editor of the Ghanaian Times. This was the very paper that I served as London correspondent before going to Budapest and Vienna. The offer came as a thunderbolt from a clear blue sky.

At first, my wife and I suspected that the offer might be a trap to get me to Accra to undergo the same or similar rigorous gymnastics at the airport in the hot sun that other former colleagues had endured. We discussed this matter endlessly. Finally, we both agreed that I would inform the diplomat that I would give my response the following day.

The diplomat was duly informed. And the next twenty-four hours, Breid made frantic calls to close friends in London, Israel, and America. They were to make discreet inquiries in Accra about whether the offer was genuine and kosher or a trap. With two small babies to care and look after, we could not afford to take any chances. After all, to have a hard time in London was certainly far preferable to languish in a hot jail, after possibly getting a few kicks and a volley of insults.

Breid's efforts were not in vain. Within three hours, all those that she contacted, seven in all, stated that to their knowledge, the offer was kosher and harmless. But they could not guarantee what might happen later on. So after due family deliberation, we were in a position to take a calculated risk and reply positively to the diplomat's request the following day. My new friend, perhaps worrying that I might use my new position to cause his recall home, thus ending the good life, was over polite, bordering on servility.

For the next two days, my wife and I awaited, with bated breath, the response from Accra. Then on the third day, my friend rang again with his newfound respect, repeating "Your Excellency," again and again as we talked. He said that he had been instructed to make first class flight arrangements from London to Accra for me, by the next week if possible, to meet with the military junta to formalize my appointment as the editor of Ghana's leading newspaper.

The next couple of days were spent by Breid and I putting my affairs in order in case the unexpected became a reality. We devised a simple code which when sent by me would indicated whether I was in trouble or not, and that if disaster had struck, she was to contact immediately her rabbi, my Methodist minister, my old and reliable friend, Edward, and my journalist friend, the editor of the influential weekly *West Africa* magazine in London. Having satisfied myself that the risk in the travel was worth taking and with the full approval and support of Breid, one Friday morning, we set off in an embassy car to Heathrow Airport. Where after the departure formalities had been completed, Breid kissed me goodbye and returned home as I flew to Accra.

For all the six and a quarter hour flight, I sat quiet, thinking and fretting. I was not at all sure whether the decision I had taken was a wise one. Apart from a few minutes chat with an Englishwoman of about thirty who was sitting on my left, I spoke with nobody. This innocent, well-meaning woman had told me that she was going to Ghana to marry a prince to whom she was engaged. I felt it my moral duty to explain to her that if even the chap was a prince, she should not expect the same or similar trappings, comforts, and luxuries that go with being a prince in her own country. Instead of being grateful to me for the sound advice that I was giving her without charging her any fee whatsoever as a lawyer, she was rather angry, although it was she who had initially asked me to tell her something about Ghana. My desire to enlighten her was motivated by altruism and by the fact that as a diplomat at the Ghana embassy, before going to Hungary and Vienna, I had been involved in settling cases of some unscrupulous young men from Ghana who, cashing in on the gullibility and ignorance of some young white women that they had met in London, had told them big lies that their fathers or uncles were kings or princes or wealthy business tycoons or landowners. Being a father myself of two small baby girls, I felt that it was absolutely wrong for any persons from my country to treat some of the white girls as I had known to happen. Sadly, the young lady who had requested my help did not take kindly to what I had to tell her.

Arriving at the Accra airport, I was warmly met by the general manager of the Ghanaian Times group and the deputy press secretary at the Castle. I sighed with much relief but still was not certain that a trap was not awaiting me. Driven to Ghana's leading hotel at that time, the Ambassador Hotel, I was relieved to be back, especially as six years earlier I had stayed in the same five-star hotel for ten weeks, all expenses paid by the government on a commission to collect and write a book on Ghana's transition into a republic.

This hotel had a particular interest to me. For I vividly recall that four years before my first stay at the hotel and before I left for England, I had walked at least on two nights on the street opposite the hotel and seen a glittering spectacle. A few rich Africans and lots of white men in immaculate black ties and dinner suits with their ladies in gorgeous, lavish gowns, and white, long gloves to the elbow, one or two of them wearing tiaras, were wining, dining, and dancing merrily. The ornate chandeliers sparkled, and the black Ghanaian hotel staff busily serving their customers bowed and scraped in their bright uniforms. And I clearly recaptured my distress as I watched this lovely and grand show, asking myself, *Whenever would I have the chance to step in this august hotel?*

As soon as I reached the hotel, I telephoned my wife and signified by the agreed code that so far, all was well and that the D-day—the interview date—was the following Monday. Naturally, I renewed my requests for maximum prayers by her, her rabbi, and my Methodist minister. A day after my arrival, I was briefed by the general manager of the newspaper group, who assured me that as the previous editors were all in jail after a good beating, I had a moral duty to accept the offer as the editor of the paper that I used to represent in London before going to Hungary. Little did this gentleman know of the fear that was gnawing in my heart about the possibility of my arrest by the military junta.

I was happy to hear the voice of my mother when I called her. She was elated but doubted whether it was wise to come back, for many people still associated me with the defunct regime, oblivious of what had happened to me in London about a year before the military coup. I assured her that with God on my side and her blessing, I would be all right.

Walking into the room for the interview was not at all easy. Sitting in front of the seven-man military junta, people who had brought the Ghana dictatorship to an abrupt, unexpected end and held power over the livelihoods and lives of millions of people, was a most terrifying experience. A couple or so of the panel carried their revolvers. One word from them and I would be marching to prison. And mind you, not the sort of British or American prison where the inmates get three lovely meals a day, comfortable beds, good medical care, color television, regular visits from family or friends or charity or social workers, exercise facilities, library, and for good behavior, even weekend family visits home.

All my inner fears were put to rest at the interview, which was a very informal affair. As for most of my adult life, I had been in the position of interviewing other people, both black and white, for jobs I was well prepared for the ordeal. However, it was all smooth sailing. The only concern of the junta was whether I would use my new position as editor of Ghana's most influential and prestigious daily newspaper to facilitate the return of the deposed president, which after the coup was high treason carrying the death penalty.

At the conclusion of the interview, the junta confirmed my appointment. I was allowed three weeks to return to London to wind up my affairs and take up my new position. So at long last, my ordeal was over. The fears that I had entertained all along were completely unjustified, thank God. I returned to the hotel on cloud nine, now beginning to understand the spiritual import of the misfortune which came as a job loss that was in reality, a blessing in disguise.

Returning to London, I gave a couple of press conferences and was interviewed by the *Evening Standard* of London about my new appointment. Breid started the preparation for our return, and by six weeks we were all in Accra, I had preceded them three weeks earlier to prepare our new home given by the military government.

Duly settled in her new home, her second visit to Ghana, Breid immediately set an impressive pace in home entertainment and hospitality which soon became the talk of the town. All visitors, both black and white, knew that at "that Breid's house, you would always get something delicious to eat." She was busily involved in caring after our two small daughters, as well as training and supervising the household staff of five—comprising a cook, maid, driver, watchman, and gardener.

Being an editor of a state newspaper during the period of military regime was an immense challenge, for it meant doing the right thing as I saw it without being accused as a former ambassador of the past regime of trying covertly to aid the resurrection of the dead regime. Many a time, I received abusive letters and telephone calls for being pro-Nkrumah. At that time, in those hectic days, when many intellectual prominent people and the masses were baying for the blood of the members and close associates of the defeated government, it was anathema and dangerous to be associated in any way with the past administration. Equally, some of my friends and colleagues from the past government felt that I had let them down and was not taking up their cause robustly enough.

With the moral support of my wife, I faced each challenge as best as I could as it came along, for I was convinced that in the end, my editorial position would be vindicated by history.

The greatest challenge came when the reports by the various committees of inquiry set by the junta on the record and activities of the members of the previous regime were published. These investigations and inquiries had been instructed to delve into the minute details of the lives of the hapless persons from the time of birth to the day of the coup. Salaries and incomes and expenditure, assets, movable and immovable, vacations, bank accounts, foreign and local, gifts and legacies—all had to be accounted for in public sittings under the glare of the blinding lights of television cameras amid the jeers and wild shouts of some members of the public.

It fell on me as an editor to review the reports, and it was a very difficult and unpleasant task. For the reports did establish that there had been massive and obscene corruption by many of the past politicians, male and female. For there was no rational explanation for the gargantuan rise in the fortunes of these politicians, many of them starting financially from point zero! Knowing well as friends many of the indicted persons, I agonized a great deal about what was the right thing to do for the nation, for future generations, and for my erstwhile friends and colleagues. After a number of discussions with my unpaid closest advisor-cum-best friend and confidant, I decided that the best policy was to take a balanced and fair position that I could live with for the rest of my life.

So at a time when to debunk and destroy the reputations of the past leaders, their wives and known mistresses, was very fashionable, I wrote a series of editorials stating that although the reports established unquestionably that the defunct administration had been knee deep in corruption ad nauseam, not all of them were corrupt and that it would be grossly unfair and a flagrant disregard of justice to tar all of them with the same brush. What happened to the nation's motto of "Freedom and Justice?" I intoned, having in mind the ears, eyes, and minds of the military junta.

Breid and I were so relieved and happy that my strident calls for moderation and fairness were heeded by the members of the military junta. For they finally brought in decrees, confiscating the assets and properties of the fallen politicians that were softer on the dispossessed men and their wives than the masses, egged on by some intellectuals and other opinion leaders, were calling for. Those were indeed very trying times for my wife, me, and the nation.

About two months after my editorial appeals for moderation and against a blanket punishment of all the members of the past government, my wife and I attended the Annual Queen's Birthday Party at the British High Commission (embassy) Residence in Accra. It was a lovely affair, with plenty of delicious English food and fine wines, rounded off with champagne. The weather was cool and pleasant. My wife and I were standing in a corner, enjoying ourselves with two delightful diplomats when we were approached by a charming English woman. She introduced herself as a lawyer and wife of one of the ex-ministers in prison. What this kind woman said next touched our hearts. She said with enormous gratitude, that she was almost in tears when she read my editorials in which I had stated that not all the former ministers were corrupt and that I had mentioned specifically her husband and a few others.

My wife and I were so happy that we affectionately kissed her, and she left. Later, on our way home after the most enjoyable event, Breid and I reflected on the days in London when we had to take straight on the chin the bad news of my dismissal by the now defunct regime. It dawned on both of us that the job loss was indeed a blessing in disguise. Why? Well, first it spared me from deep public humiliation and certain imprisonment. Secondly, it placed me in a position by which, and through which, I was able to save the lives of a number of luckless and hapless people, and at the very least, bring solace and peace to many families in dire straits and ameliorate their pain and suffering. I am absolutely convinced that it was by divine intervention that the unwelcome misfortune struck us about nine months before the military coup. It was a huge blessing dressed as a nasty misfortune.

Musa, Drive Him Out

All the major religions teach that not only is it right to always do the right thing, but also that whatever we do comes back to us in one form or another. In the Hindu religion, it is called the law of karma. The Bible is replete with admonishments to do the right thing, and that whatever a man sows, so shall he reap. Islam similarly states that one cannot escape the consequences of one's actions.

Indeed, outside the realm of religion, the same principle exists in the field of science. Newton's third law of motion states, "To every action, there is an equal and opposite reaction." And come to think of it, this should not be all that surprising. How can any rational human being expect to throw a ball at a wall and for the ball not come back to him? Or expect to plant potatoes and harvest wheat? Even allowing for possible mutations, it is normally what is sowed or planted that is harvested in multiple folds. As I grow older and wiser, I realize how true, immutable, and inescapable this principle is even on a daily basis. The story of my interaction several years ago with an Englishman in my hometown, Agona Swedru, may be found seriocomic, but also helps to underline the truth of Newton's law even in the spiritual world.

One evening, after about four years at Achimota, I decided during the Easter vacation to go to the part of the town where the white people lived. It was called the Bungalows because all the houses were bungalows of one or two bedrooms. Compared with the houses of the local people, the bungalows looked grand and smart, with all the modern amenities available which were not accessible to the local people.

In theory, although it was not designated as a "white only area," as only those occupying certain high government positions could live there, in practice, it had become a "white only area." For no Africans at that time held any senior government positions because they were not university graduates, and the few British university-educated men recently returned from Great Britain, were told that although they had the necessary degrees for the positions, they had to wait because they did not have the relevant experience to hold the jobs! So although there was no official racial discrimination in West Africa as existed in East and South Africa, in reality, it did exist, albeit not on a grand scale. For the thick Tropical forests, the hot humid climate, and the malaria made West Africa not ideal destination of choice for white sellers.

Indeed, local conditions were considered so deleterious to white people that colonial civil servants and other expatriate employees from Britain were allowed to retire at age forty-five and discouraged from bringing their wives to Ghana and other West African countries. The prevalence of a good number of Ghanaians and other West Africans of biracial origin or with solid British names can easily be understood. For West Africa was then known as the "white man's grave," due to the very high mortality rates over short periods among European missionaries, public servants, teachers, and adventurers.

At Achimota, as students, we had been told and taught by our English masters and mistresses to think for ourselves and be ready to express our views without fear or hesitation so long as it was done politely and respectfully. It had been drummed into our heads that all people are endowed with the same or similar basic intelligence or capabilities and that no groups of people or race were superior to others. At a time in the history of the world, when racism was the standard practice and way of life in Europe and America, openly supported without batting an eyelid by high church men, these ideas were indeed revolutionary. Looking back, I am amazed at how avant-garde, enlightened, and futuristic the British teachers at Achimota were. They were indeed a great credit and asset to their nation.

About four years after I entered Achimota, I decided one day to put to the test some of the sound antiracism ideas that had been inculcated in me. One Wednesday evening, while on Easter holidays, I dressed smartly in my standard white shorts and shirt, put on my Achimota sandals and said prayers for about ten minutes, for I was going on a venture that indeed needed spiritual support.

Swedru then did not have a public library, art gallery, museum, or community center. So I spent my holidays reading and reading till I got bored and tired. Indeed, apart from my daily visits to the local Methodist bookstore to browse through some of the books and discuss current affairs with the store manager, there was nothing else to do or nowhere else to go.

Furthermore, I needed money badly as my dear mother was not in a position to give me pocket money in addition to the necessary financial outlays on my education. So my determination to seek a vacation job, however modest, was driven by necessity rather than by choice.

I walked the two or three miles from my mother's home, through the bush to the local radio station. I sat on the concrete steps for a few minutes to gather my breath. Then I crossed the road to the bungalow where I had been told the white engineer who was the local representative of the public works department of the colonial government was living.

It was a lucky day for me. For as I approached his residence, I saw a white man on the patio of the house drinking what later I learnt was gin and tonic. It was an evening favorite of white expatriates in those days and even now. My mission was to go and plead for a vacation job. It is true that I had not made a previous appointment with him, but that was normal and nothing unusual those days and even now to some extent. Visitors, black and white, call on "big shots," namely doctors, teachers, editors, engineers, lawyers, academics, government ministers, and senior civil servants without appointment, hoping to be lucky!

I approached the white Englishman with trepidation. He could have been Welsh or Scottish or English, but those days and generally even now, a white Briton is called an Englishman, irrespective of whether he is Irish, Scottish, Welsh, or English.

The gentleman was tall, blond, and sported a small moustache. He was wearing a long sleeves white shirt and white trousers tucked into mosquito boots. For by the time I got there, the dusk was setting in and mosquitoes were beginning to make their presence felt.

With the conviction that my Achimota training would see me through, I approached the white man. I saluted him, bowing slightly then said, "Sir, I am sorry to bother you, but I have come to discuss something with you." He looked at me with a wry smile, then to my astonishment, said, "You, small boy, come to discuss something with me?" Next he shouted, "Musa, get him out."

From nowhere, his manservant, a tall hefty, barefooted man wearing a long white gown, suddenly appeared with a big stick toward me, shouting in the local Fanti language, "Get out, you silly, cheeky, small boy. Don't you fear the white man? Don't you know that the white people rule the world? Get out now!"

I ran in a way that I had never before ever done. And crossing the street to the radio station, I was nearly hit by a car driven by a Ghanaian taking his white boss home. As I sat again at the steps of the radio station to get my breath back, I was really sad that my first direct encounter with a white man on a one-on-one basis had ended so unexpectedly and so negatively.

I did not cry but was on the verge of doing so. Repeating to myself again and again, "White people are bad, really bad." I just could not figure out what had gone wrong. For all that I had done was to try to implement some of the ideas and patterns of behavior that had been inculcated in me by my white teachers, both male and female at Achimota.

The more I reviewed my predicament, the greater my conviction that white people are bad and that those at Achimota were rather the exception to the rule became. In retrospect, I must confess that it took me some time to get over this humiliation and to come to the more realistic and rational conviction that rather white people, like those at Achimota, are good and that the bad ones, like my tormentor, were rather the tiny minority, completely unreflective of the overwhelming majority.

At home, I was too embarrassed and ashamed to tell my mother and aunts what had happened. I only stated, "My mission was not successful." As there were no physical signs on me of what had transpired, I was able to keep my secret to myself. Soon, the vacation was over, and I returned to Achimota to continue the good life, getting the best of education then available from some of the best English teachers that Great Britain could produce.

About twenty-five years after this episode and having gone through many years of a rather pleasant and fulfilling life in Britain, Europe, and Ghana, I had become a government minister, following the election victory of the political party of which I was a member. Representing my hometown as a member of Parliament, I had been appointed as the deputy minister of health. I enjoyed very much my tenure of fifteen months at the health ministry. Among other things, as I had failed to become a doctor, as my initial ambition was, it was rather thrilling and uplifting that I was now in a position to deal with the concerns, issues, and problems of doctors and surgeons, both black and white. The latter were mostly from Britain and Eastern Europe.

Again and again, I could not but smile inwardly when former college mates, now successful doctors or surgeons, came to me with problems to address. For some of them were not all that sympathetic to me when I fell by the wayside a few years earlier, when we were all endeavoring to be doctors, and thus be members of the noblest profession on earth bar the priesthood.

My promotion and transfer to the Ministry (Department) of Lands and Mineral Resources, following a cabinet reshuffle was a bittersweet moment for me, for I really enjoyed my work with doctors, civil servants, and patients. To me, dealing with human beings was more enjoyable, more rewarding, and more self-satisfying than dealing with diamonds, gold, bauxite, and forests.

Admittedly, most of the staff at the ministry head office in ACCRA was happy to see me back. For I was considered to be an overzealous, interfering minister who asked too many questions and had the nasty, unwelcome habit of paying unscheduled visits to hospitals and pharmacies to check what they were doing or not doing.

At the Ministry of Lands and Natural Resources, no sooner had I settled in than I was flooded with petitions and requests for gold or diamond digging licenses. They came mostly from rich Ghanaians and British businessmen. One Wednesday afternoon, after a good kosher lunch with my wife followed by a brief forty minutes siesta, I returned to my office. The day was rather hotter than usual, with the humidity rather high. About half an hour after settling in, my private secretary, Kwame, called in and said, "Mr. Minister, a certain old, white man wants to see you."

"Has he got an appointment?" I asked.

"No, sir," he replied politely.

For a moment, I was silent, and then I said, "Bring him in, but ensure that he does not stay for more than fifteen minutes as I am expecting the chairman of my local constituency party. You remember?"

"Yes, Mr. Minister." And with that, he bowed out, and in a matter of minutes, came in followed by the visitor. He looked about sixty and had the sort of dark tan usually associated with white men who have lived in the tropics for many years. His hair was grey, and he walked with a slight stoop. He wore a smart, light brown suit, complemented with a white shirt and polished brown shoes. With his almost white moustache, he looked the standard middle-class English gentleman.

As I stood up to welcome him, he said, "Mr. Minister, thank you so much for seeing me without an appointment, just as I expected."

I sat him down and called for a cup of tea for him as he introduced himself. Then I asked him "Well, welcome to my modest office, what I can do for you, my friend?"

"Mr. Minister, I have a major problem that all my friends tell me that you can solve. For they tell me that you are a decent, honest gentleman who is fair to all and sundry, irrespective of race or color. From what I hear, sir, you are incorruptible and have a charming, white wife, always helping white women who have problems or difficulties."

I smiled wanly and, looking directly at him, asked, "So what is the problem?"

Then looking rather sad, he narrated as follows: "I have been in Ghana for over thirty years as a government employee in the Department of Public Works, and after retiring, I decided to go into diamond mining as I am an engineer by profession." I listened intently to him. He continued, "Sir, I have spent a lot of money on traditional drinks, all to no avail."

"I suppose by the traditional drinks, you mean bribes, right?"

"Yes, Mr. Minister, and still nothing to show for all that expenditure, except for a lot of aggro and lies." He paused briefly, and then, clearing his throat, continued, "It is always the same story after I have parted with the money asked for. My friend, I tried hard but it did not go through, I am sorry. Following changes at the Ministry, things are not as easy as before.

"This is what they invariably tell me after they have taken and squandered my money. Sir, I am really tired and frustrated and decided that I would take the bull by the horns and come to you. Hence, my unscheduled visit this afternoon. Please, accept my heartfelt apologies."

I sighed and said, "What a shame, some of my people are really bad and also greedy. After all the expensive official campaign nationwide against corruption, with the official slogan 'Zero Tolerance for Corruption,' many are still at it. They are completely oblivious of the message and its moral and economic implications. Hmmm!"

Then I asked him about where he had served in Ghana. He replied with utter satisfaction, "Cape Coast, Saltpond, Agona Swedru, Winneba, all in the central region. Then for my last seven years, I was in Ashanti region. I retired from the colonial service with a clean record having served Britain and Ghana to the best of my abilities. Sir, I have even brought the letter of commendation from the Ghanaian head of my department when I retired. You may have a look at it, Mr. Minister."

He was pulling it from his jacket's breast pocket, when I interjected, "Don't bother, I believe you." He paused for a few seconds and then continued, "Sir, I know that you have the power to help me, and I hope that you do so. I am in your hands as the Ghanaian saying goes, sir."

As he spoke, I realized that he was the same white man that twenty-five years or so ago that had ordered his male servant, Musa, to chase me like a dog from his residence. A small, still voice kept telling me, "Yes! This is the guy. He is the same man, no other."

To be 100 percent sure about what was rambling through my head, I asked him about what years he was in Swedru and Winneba. His response to both questions confirmed without any shadow of a doubt that indeed, the man sitting humbly before me was indeed the man that I had had a brief interaction with about a quarter of a century ago.

Again and again, I asked myself, *Should I order my police escort sitting in my secretary's office to come in and chase him out with his baton? Should I reveal my true identity to him as the same "small boy" that he rudely ordered to be flushed out? Should I show him power as now, he was at the receiving end, and I was the one in control of the situation?*

While these questions and ideas rushed through my mind, I kept hearing another voice saying clearly, "Hey, Joseph, don't be a hypocrite. You call yourself a Christian and a believer in God, and here you are, wanting to inflict pain and suffering on a poor, innocent white man. Why? What purpose is served by your adding to his predicament in his old age by paying him back in the same coin? The fact that he is already here, sitting plaintively before you, pleading for help should be sufficient satisfaction for you. Unless you wish to give in to your atavistic, sadistic instincts and make him squirm and suffer. And what useful purpose would it serve anyway, by seeing him in emotional turmoil? Come on, you should rationally balance his awful behavior with the extremely nice, good treatment and benevolent behavior that you have received for decades from many white people. The fact that this man sitting before you was bad and awful does not mean that they are all like that. What about the millions of white men and women who, defying the covert and overt ridicule and opprobrium of their own bigoted people, have valiantly over the years stood up for the cause of Africans and Asians and fearlessly opposed racism, colonial exploitation and reprehensible and untoward behavior and utterances by their own kith and kin?"

For a few moments, I was lost in thought. Then I pulled myself together and called in the chief of staff of the ministry. Mr. John Prah was of medium height and build. Highly educated and principled, he was a British-trained civil servant of the old school. He was a lay preacher in his local Methodist church in Accra and was held in very high esteem by all who knew him. Ever so polite, professional, and loyal, he was nevertheless inscrutable. He was at ease with all ministers as they came and went. You could never tell what he really thought deep down or felt about any issue, apart from the official, professional advice that he was giving.

I asked my secretary to take my white visitor to his office to wait for a few minutes. When he left, I discussed the application of my visitor, and the civil servant agreed with me that the application should be granted. I called for the relevant file, and having given it a quick read, there and then approved my visitor's request. Having duly signed it, I affixed my official stamp on it. Next, I called in my secretary and asked him to make a photocopy of the approval note for the records. Then I called in my visitor. The few minutes that he had spent in the secretary's office seemed to have drained him, for he looked rather tense and stressed.

He sat before me hoping for the best but prepared for the worst. He looked calmly at me as I smiled at him. Suddenly, I said, "Well, my friend, your application has been approved by me, and this is your approval note. Good luck for the future." He smiled broadly as if he had won a big prize on the British Premium Bonds lottery. Standing up, he thanked me profusely and gave me a vigorous handshake. "You may go now, my friend, and by the way, no traditional drinks needed." He bowed respectfully and was led to his car by my secretary. And that was the last that I saw of him. About a week after his visit, I received a most touching letter of gratitude from him, signed, "Yours Ever, Peter Watson."

Exactly a year after Peter's visit, there was a military coup in Ghana, and the democratically elected government of which I was a member as a deputy minister was overthrown, and all the ministers were arrested. We were roughed up, not beaten, but subjected to a volley of insults and humiliation. Locked up in the notorious Ussher Fort Prison in Accra for fifteen horrendous months, I lived in the first few days on food worse than what my wife's seven cats used to eat. With close family members taking a low profile for obvious reasons and with only my wife endowed with the courage to visit me in prison, it was a huge relief to receive a letter from outside the prison.

About ten days after my arrest, a senior officer gave me a letter from Peter. Of course, it had been opened first by the authorities and read before handing it over to me. The letter was most heartwarming. In it, Peter expressed his shock and sadness at my predicament and how he had failed at least on three occasions to get a permit to visit me in prison from the attorney-general's office because he was not a close family relation. To my utter delight and surprise, he wrote also that he had, after determined efforts, found my wife and children in their new home at Labone, near the Residence of the British Ambassador and gone there to commiserate with them and given them a thousand dollars as a token appreciation for what I had done for him. As I read and reread the letter, I was so happy that I had not ever divulged to Peter my true identity.

To many people, a thousand dollars may not sound all that great. But a thousand American dollars was in those days a fortune in Ghana, especially as the bank accounts of all the ministers and their wives were frozen by military decree! What Peter did for me in my hour of utter anguish and suffering, deserted by former friends and relatives, made up a thousand times for the little running that he had unknowingly put me through twenty-five or so years previously.

Our Guardian Angel

In Ghana, as in many countries the world over, public life carries with it immense esteem in the eyes of fellow citizens, a lot of perks, and enormous prestige and power to do good or bad. Admittedly, it is not as well paid as in the private sector, but this deficiency is made up for by the unique privileges attached to public life, especially at the higher echelons. Whether the individual holding a position of public trust uses it for personal enrichment and aggrandizement or for the improvement of the whole population is another matter.

However, one major advantage that politicians in the developed countries have over those from the less developed countries is that they do not have to fret over the possibility of sudden, unexpected military coups scuppering their positions and livelihoods.

This story demonstrates the enormous dangers attached to public political office in developing countries.

One Saturday morning, at about eleven, my wife was getting ready for the beach as she always did on Saturdays and Sundays. As I had no engagement in my constituency, I decided to join them for the ride. The maid and the driver were already waiting for us.

I walked to the sitting room and stood next to the family radio and television. The driver came to me and said, "Master, somebody wants to see you. He says that it is urgent."

Although to call at my official residence on the Sabbath day without an appointment was nothing unusual, I was rather put off as we were about to leave for the beach.

"Bring him in," I told the driver. In a few minutes, he returned, followed by a slim, tallish man of about twenty-seven or twenty-eight. He looked charming and decent.

Sitting him down, I asked him how I could be of help to him. Nervously, he began as follows, "Honorable Minister, I am very sorry to bother you this morning, but I have a big problem."

"What is it?" I asked.

"Well, Mr. Minister, I returned from the Soviet Union a couple of weeks ago where I had studied criminology and prison administration. I had been offered an appointment by the government as a senior prison officer"

"Then?" I inquired.

"Sir, since my arrival, the promised furnished two-bedroom bungalow has not materialized. My wife who is from Moscow and our little son are suffering badly. They cannot sleep and have terrible mosquito bites all over their bodies. Sir, it is a nightmare for them, and I fear they may collapse or die from malaria."

He continued, "Sir, our position is desperate, and I have been trying to trace the deputy speaker of Parliament, who is a relative of mine, whether he can help us. My wife and son keep crying often, and I am distraught with depression and anxiety. They promised me a nice house, but when we came, we were given all sorts of excuses why the house was not available. Now we are in a terrible one-bedroom shack that is bad and completely unsuitable. In Moscow, we had a lovely modest apartment, and here we are in my own country, without somewhere decent to lay our heads."

Listening carefully, I intoned, "This reflects badly on our country and its people. Our officials should think well and thoroughly before attracting needed public sector staff with promises that they cannot fulfill."

The little dialogue between us was going on when Breid walked in and joined. She advised that as the request of the young man was rather important and urgent, it must be given proper hearing the following morning, at about eleven. Our two daughters, already in their swimming costumes, were itching to go to the car and take their seats. So while our visitor walked away, we drove off to the beach and had a lovely afternoon in the warm tropical sea.

The following day, as agreed, our visitor turned up at the precise time. With the maid supervising our daughters in their Wendy house in the garden, Breid and I sat down with our friends, for he was now accompanied by his Russian wife and a small son of about five years. Breid and I had one look at both mother and son and were shocked and distressed to see the numerous blotches on their faces and hands from mosquito bites. Breid immediately arranged for the little boy to be washed and groomed by the mother in our bathroom, while we continued the conversation with our Ghanaian friend. Next, we all had a lovely brunch prepared by the cook on the instructions of Breid. What our good friend, John, told us was a repeat of what he had told us the previous day, but with more details and passion.

Breid and I had no choice after listening to his story but to promise to help. "Madam, I beg you, in the name of God, to help us, for my family are suffering." Assured by us of our determination and ability to help solve his housing problem, John left with his family. We could notice a new spring in John's step as he walked away. Their stay, including the brunch time, had lasted about one and a half hours.

When they left, Breid and I agonized about how we were going to help them as promised. I began to realize that perhaps I had overreached myself in giving the under taking to help. Then in a flash, Breid reminded me about the furnished bungalows on the compound of the Ridge Hospital in Accra, meant for visiting doctors or foreign doctors on their arrival in Accra on their way to their stations up country. This hospital, which was originally called the "European Hospital Ridge" during colonial times, had been renamed the Ridge Hospital in 1948, immediately after the riots and political upheavals in February of that year. On a number of occasions, my wife had gone there to visit white patients who had no friends or relatives to visit them. So she had a pretty good idea of the layout of the hospital. With her usual enthusiasm and concern for those in distress, she had made it her business to get involved with the social and humanitarian aspects of my work as deputy minister (secretary) of health.

But unfortunately for John and his family, at the time of their call, I had been moved from the Ministry of Health to that of Lands and Mineral Resources. Diamonds, gold, bauxite, manganese, and state or federal lands had replaced medicines, surgical equipment, and hospitals. So my influence or power over the health ministry and its assets were practically zero.

Still, the following morning, when I went to my office, I called my successor at health and inquired about the availability of any of the bungalows at Ridge. He undertook to make the relevant inquiries and call me in an hour's time. This he did but with bad news! "My brother, they are all booked for the next eight months, sorry. I really wished that I could help. See you soon, cheers, don't forget Tuesday's meeting." My heart sank as he spoke, for it was beginning to dawn on me that I had bitten more than I could chew. I had given a promise that I was not in the position to fulfill, and in so doing, had committed the same sin that I had, to John's face, accused others of. I did not know what to do next.

The next few weeks were unnerving for me. For every morning, at about eleven, John would call at my office, smartly dressed in his prison officer uniform with a baton under his armpit. He would smile sadly and salute then say, "Chief, I just came to remind you. We are suffering desperately."

I would then say, "John, don't worry, I am working on it. I will do my best, greetings to your wife and son, goodbye." He salutes, then walks away. I was anxious to assist him as promised, but the truth of the matter was that I was at my wit's end on how I was going to achieve this. His visits became so regular that some of my office staff thought that he was a relative of mine or possibly a brother or relative of a mistress of mine.

While John pestered me at the office, Breid also kept reminding me often about the plight of John and his family and our promise to help them. Subjected regularly to the two pronged pressures, I felt frustrated as I could not do much to redeem my promise. On a number of times, I felt like giving up, but an inner still voice kept telling me, "Don't give up, don't give up, you must see this thing through to the end, the very bitter end." As I listened to this voice, in utter desperation, I often asked myself, "Why, why did you put yourself in this odd situation? What or who made you give a promise that you were in no way to fulfill?" I must confess that on at least on one or two occasions, I was tempted to drive my friend and tormentor away with a lie that I was very busy. In fact, on one occasion, when my private secretary came to my office to inform me that John was in, I told him to tell him that I was at a meeting. As this was the standard excuse for top officials or government ministers who did not want to see unscheduled visitors, my secretary smiled, bowed politely, and went back to his office. Just as he resumed his work, I had a prick of conscience and called him back. "Let the guy in when he comes! I have changed my mind."

"Yes, sir," he responded with the same loyalty as before. And he went away.

One Friday, in, I think, the second week, I was so angry and fed up with the ridiculous position that I had put myself in that I told Breid, who had been a party to the promise that I was giving up, "I really must eat my words and accept defeat."

"No, never, you just cannot do that. This young woman is far from home, knows nobody here, speaks no English, and they are in dire straits. Darling, we must do the right thing and help them … How you do it is your responsibility as a minister of the republic. You must find a way out."

"But he is making my life hell, unbearable!"

"Well, Joseph, a promise is a promise, and you can do it if you really want to. You remember the old saying 'Where there is a will, there is a way,' right?"

I listened but could say nothing meaningful in response.

About three weeks into my now established regular interaction with John, just before he came to my office, I had a flash of inspiration. I recalled that at the first briefing by the permanent secretary (chief of staff) of the ministry, he had told me that the ministry of lands and mineral resources had three furnished four-bedroom staffed houses in the residential area close to the "English" or Ridge Church. They were meant for visiting VIPs and members of committees or boards under the ministry who were attending meetings from outside the capital.

"Eureka," I shouted to myself. I felt that I had cracked the problem. So before John walked in, I went to the office of the chief of staff and sat on his lovely green sofa.

"Chief, sorry to intrude, but I have I have a big problem," I began.

The quaint, professional, top civil servant smiled politely and said, "You of all people?"

"Yes, sir." Although he was almost my father's age, brought up in a tradition in which age is revered, I always gave him the due respect, irrespective of the fact that in rank, I was higher than he was.

Over the months, Mr. Prah and I had become good friends as we had much in common. We were both Methodists, went to the same church where he was an elder and occasional lay preacher, and were both Fantis from the coast, the first tribe in Ghana to interact with the white people coming from Europe. Furthermore, on the few occasions that Breid sent my lunch to the office when I could not go home for one reason or another, I readily invited him to join me in a delicious kosher meal. Always, before we started our meal, looking at the polished and shining silver tray and cutlery, he would remark, "Look at how the white lady does things, just look at this." Then he would say a little prayer of thanks for God's boundless mercies and blessings.

My relations with Mr. Prah being rather informal, he listened carefully as I narrated my story. In brief, I told him about how and when John had first called at our home and the problem that he had saddled me with, all because I had opened my big mouth and made a promise that I was in no position to redeem. I pleaded with him to get me one of the official houses, if necessary, I would pay the rent for the period that John and his family occupied it. "Chief, please try and help me, for it is becoming very difficult for my wife and me."

From studying his demeanor, I could guess that he hardly believed me. For here was a government minister urgently requesting a house to be released from the housing pool for VIPs to give to a young man that the minister stated was not a friend or relative or not romantically connected to a sister or aunt or close friend of the man in question.

When I finished speaking, he smiled and said, "Mr. Minister, the question of rent does not come in at all. The issue is one of availability."

He paused and then said, "Let me check with protocol." There and then, in my presence, he rang the protocol officer and inquired whether any of the houses were free. While he talked, I said a brief prayer. Next, he put down the telephone receiver and said, "Mr. Minister, good news. House number 7 is vacant. The rest are booked for the next two months." I thanked him heartily and left his office after hearing him give instructions that the house should be ready for occupation by the following morning, at the latest by ten.

Returning to my office, I immediately telephoned my wife with the excellent news. She was elated and so happy; I felt that I was walking on the moon, for I could now face the young man and look at him directly, man-to-man, eyeball-to-eyeball, without having to tell a whopping lie. So when John came in again, I gave him the good news. He was so excited and delirious with happiness that the baton under his armpit fell to the carpet in the office. I told him that he could stay in the house till he was given the furnished housing promised by the prison authorities. There was no rent or utility bills to pay. Just move in and look after his family. He saluted smartly, shook my hand firmly, and left as a happy and relieved family man. He could now face his Russian wife without more excuses and apologies. That was the last time that I set eyes on John in my office.

At home, Breid was overjoyed with the news and kept repeating, "I knew all along that you would pull it through. Never had the slightest doubts about this. Well done, darling, well done!" I looked at her, hugged her, and said, "But for you, I would have given up. For indeed it came to a point where as the Holy Bible states, 'The spirit is willing, but the flesh is weak.'"

Later in the evening, Breid got our driver to take her to the house. She inspected the place and asked for extra cleaning and polishing to be done here and there to meet her own high standards. Not content with herself, she next went and did some grocery shopping from the most prestigious store in Accra, remembering to include food items favored by her Jewish people.

The following morning, after dropping our daughters at the international school, she went with our maid to the deplorable and shabby room of John and his family and collected their personal belongings. Then the mother and son accompanied Breid in the car to their new home. They were warmly welcomed by the staff. Breid then supervised the packing of the groceries into the fridge and deep freezer. Nina was so happy she said something to her son in Russian that registered her utter delight and happiness. As she spoke no English, the happy and bright glow on her face adequately expressed what she felt. Still she was able to muster enough English to repeat, "Thank you very much, madam. Very good."

The following morning, as by Ghanaian custom, John came to our home and profusely expressed their gratitude to Breid and me. We were so delighted that in our own modest way, we had been able to make a difference in their lives. At the very least, we had added a modicum of happiness to their rather challenging life. We waved goodbye to John and his family and did not see them again.

Life as a minister continued at a hectic pace. Each day was filled with all sorts of requests for money, help for pregnant wives, or ailing mothers. In addition, one had to cope with numerous telephone calls, scheduled and unscheduled visits from both local and foreign men and women, a number of meetings, and also read thick files and reports. There was little or no time to think of the past. With the local media often singing the praises of our administration and with the masses expressing on a grand scale their admiration of the sagacity, wisdom, and great work of the national leadership, and with the high religious leaders openly praying that the government should last many decades, no one in government ever dreamed that in a matter of a few months, a catastrophic event of enormous historic importance was going to hit the country. None of the prophets or seers or diviners or spiritualists were able to forecast what was looming on the horizon.

Well, on that fateful day, January 13, 1972, the democratically elected government was overthrown, and all of us, government ministers and senior party officials, were arrested. We were not beaten but were subjected to a fusillade of abuse and insults. After two hours in the police station near the residence of the British High Commissioner (ambassador) in Accra, I was moved with other colleagues in a commandeered bus to the Ussher Fort Prison in Accra. This is a formidable old slave fort built in the eighteenth century by the Danes but later on taken over by the British. It was then used as a prison for hardened criminals.

On our way to the prison, my fellow ex-ministers sung hymns till our voices were hoarse, then ended at our new residence at about eight in the night. We were all sitting on the hard benches, dejected and tongue-tied. I just did not know what was happening or why. Meditating on my predicament, I began to doze intermittingly. In a state half-dozing and half-awake, I felt that somebody was shaking my right knee. Opening my eyes, I saw standing before me a tall, young man in mufti. Lo and behold, it was the same man that my wife and I had helped a year or so past. Yes, it was him all right, but this time, not in his smart, khaki uniform. My heart must have missed a beat when he said with a smile, "Chief, don't worry. I am in charge here and will look after you. I have already gone to see madam and the children, and they are all right. Don't worry!" With the sounds of gunfire outside and masses of people dancing excitedly and jubilating loudly in the night at our downfall and calling for our blood, the words of John were so soothing and so warmly reassuring that they sounded as if coming from a saint. I stood to attention as he shook my hand and went away to give orders to his warders.

As he walked away, I reflected on the days when he unknowingly used to annoy me by his regular visits and the couple of occasions when I was really tempted to drive him away or tell him that I could not keep the promise that we had made to him

For the fifteen horrendous months that I was in political detention in Ussher Fort, my life was literally in the hands of John. For as the head of the prison, he could order any of his truncheon carrying warders to harass me and others by ordering them to ransack our personal belongings because we were not allowed to keep anything apart from the Holy Bible. And from stories told by previous political prisoners, victims of an earlier military coup, the warders delighted in jeering, sneering, and humiliating their past political leaders and ministers. They appeared to revel to their hearts' content in their newfound power over the past high and mighty.

To the best of his ability and as far as the rules permitted, John treated me like a king. Against the prison rules, he frequently brought me letters and news from my wife and children. They were a most welcome relief from the tedium of thinking all that time about my wife and children and what was going to happen to us. Would it be freedom or the firing squad, or at best a long period of incarceration?

Although as the boss, John was not subject to a search by any prison staff, he still took precautions when bringing news or letters to me. Just as he approached my bed, he would order the warder accompanying him to go to his office to make a telephone call or search for a file that he well knew was not in his office. That gave him a few precious minutes to interact with me and give me badly needed reassurance. On a few occasions, he even brought me a piece of fruit cake from my wife. Somehow, it tasted better than before I went to prison!

To minimize the tedium and boredom of my detention, John even brought me paperback novels by Russian writers such as Pushkin and Tolstoy. The big pockets of his elegant khaki jacket had room for whatever he brought me. John was the ideal conduit for me to send letters and messages to my wife and children, although the latter, with childish innocence, thought, "Daddy had gone to a big boarding school." For on a few occasions, during visits with their mother, they saw us exercising in the prison compound.

Anytime John came on his regular morning inspections, we all stood to attention. But it was noticeable to fellow inmates how well and friendly John treated me as if I was his boss. Indeed, he still called me Chief although I was now under him.

My fellow colleagues duly noticed how nicely he dealt with me. This was a man that we all feared, for he could make our lives a living hell if he wanted to. Finally, my friends, in an effort to fathom out the relationship between John and me, one sultry night after prayers, asked me the rationale for his special attitude to me. It was then that I told them the story of how about a year or so ago, John had come to our home with his long and sad story, and how Breid and I had done our little bit to ameliorate the conditions of his family. They all listened to me carefully, nodding or shaking their heads in subdued amazement and silence.

About two weeks after the coup, Breid had to move from the comfortable government house that I occupied as a minister. She was in a desperate situation as she had nowhere to go because both our houses were rented out. Quickly, she negotiated with the tenant of our house near the residence of the British High Commissioner in Accra. The Danish tenant was most reasonable and agreed to leave on three weeks' notice instead of three months as mandated by the lease agreement.

Ironically, it was the man that Breid and I had helped with his housing problem just about a year ago that came to the assistance of Breid. He was now the one helping Breid and her daughters with their housing problem. Admittedly, much of the physical moving was done by a family friend from the United States embassy, but the role of John cannot be ignored. In a matter of just over a year, the roles had been reversed. Breid was the underdog and John the top dog, metaphorically speaking.

After fifteen very distressing and harrowing months, we were released in commemoration of the fifteenth year of the independence of the country. I was driven home by Breid in her newly acquired battered Volkswagen car. She drove me and our daughters to the office of the attorney-general. There, after all the ex-prisoners had signed bonds to the effect that we would not engage in politics again, we drove home. It was a fantastic homecoming that I remember to this day

A day following my release, John and his wife and little son called with flowers, bread, and salami. At a time when most friends, both black and white, were nowhere to be found, and at a time when even family and relatives were taking a low profile and avoiding us like the plaque, the noble gesture of John and Natasia was very touching.

For the next two weeks, they called on us about twice a week, especially at weekends. And it was a pleasure talking about the good old days.

Then one evening, they came with bad, disturbing news. John had been made to resign the previous day on grounds of favoritism to political prisoners. The authorities could not conclusively prove that he had specifically broken any prison rules or regulations. All the evidence was circumstantial and could not result in dismissal. So our family friend, John, left the prison service with a clear record, albeit under a cloud. As I had just come from prison, there was not much that Breid and I could do for them apart from a modest donation and plenty moral support. But a week after of his enforced resignation, a fishing boat on its way to Israel docked at the Tema harbor. It left on a Thursday night about midnight, after delaying its departure by two hours. The ship carried a heavy cargo of fish and three unscheduled passengers. They were a Russian, a Jewish mother, her Jewish son, and her husband. In Israel, John studied law and became a lawyer. Natasia trained as a caterer, and they settled in Zimbabwe where John got a job as a magistrate. That was the last time that Breid and I heard of our former savior and guardian angel and his family.

Policia, Please Get Me Out

When my wife and I are on vacation or holidays, we try to be together as much as possible, but sometimes, we take different approaches to enjoying the holidays. Being a psychologist, she likes to spend as much time as possible watching people. This involves talking with many people, studying them, and soaking in the sun to get a good tan. Off course, she always has time for art galleries, churches, and historic sites. Being an African with a God-given tan and having soaked enough sunshine to keep me going till eternity, I prefer to spend more time walking about, visiting old historic buildings, museums, and major centers of learning and gigantic engineering constructions. Although the buildings, being inanimate objects, do not talk with me, they have their own way of interacting with me. The difference between us in our approach to what constitutes a good vacation is highlighted in the incident which is narrated here.

A few years ago, we went to Portugal on holidays. I had been there once before on business and had been struck by the fact that about five centuries ago, that country was one of the "superpowers" of the world and that the Portuguese were the first Europeans to construct a concrete structure in Africa. It was at a small town on the coast of present-day Ghana and is called Elmina Castle. The Portuguese adventurers had been attracted to the coast of Ghana because of the gold which they found there and in the surrounding villages. They named the town the Mine of Gold, which it still bears. The trade in gold and diamonds had later drifted into trade in human beings, thus laying the foundations of the Transatlantic Slave Trade. Indeed, in the early part of the sixteenth century, there were more black people than white in the capital, Lisbon. So our visit to the historic city meant a great deal to me.

On a bright summer Thursday, with two days already spent, I decided to visit some historic buildings in Lisbon, from where centuries ago Portugal had ruled its colonies situated in Africa and Asia. So on one bright morning at about ten, I said goodbye to my wife and set out for Lisbon. Before leaving, my wife had arranged for us to have dinner with a fine Dutch couple that we had met with at the hotel and had struck a warm friendship.

My train journey to Lisbon was uneventful. As soon as I reached the city center, I started on my assignment. The museums and galleries and historic buildings were on my list. The weather was good, and I enjoyed the day immensely, walking about and taking a few photographs. Having done as much as I could, I dropped at a restaurant that I came across and had a lovely meal to charge my batteries for the rest of the day before returning to the hotel. While walking toward the center of the city, I came across a Mormon church with its doors wide open. I recalled that about ten years earlier, I had visited the Mormon church in Salt Lake City, Utah, and had been most impressed with the church, its magnificent lawns, and majestic, awe-inspiring interior. As I entered the church, vivid memories of my Salt Lake visit rushed through my mind.

When I entered the church, I heard two male American voices near where the mighty pipe organ was. I did not see them, but they sounded to me as being in their mid or late twenties. From where I was sitting, I could not hear distinctly what they were saying. After meditating and then praying for some time, I must have dozed off, for I could not hear them anymore. When I opened my eyes, I resumed my tour of the church and then stopped and prayed. I felt that I had taken in as much as I could. Then I began to walk toward the door. To my surprise, the door was locked, so I tried to find another door to exit, all to no avail. I tried again to find a way out but was unsuccessful. As time went on, I was beginning to panic. I prayed again and then began banging at the door, shouting loudly, "*Policia*, please get me out, I am inside the church!" The banging continued with brief interludes of rest. But there was no response at all. Only the voices of women could be heard by me. They listened, talked animatedly in their language, then walked way. I was starting to sweat profusely. As this incident happened before the advent of mobile phones, there was no way for me to get in touch with my wife.

I rested for some time, then resumed with my efforts to be heard outside, but the reaction was the same. People would hear me and chat among themselves; then nothing happened. Much as I was anxious about my predicament, I was also aware that if I depleted my energies with more excitement and shouting, I might faint and possibly end in a coma; and if help did not come in time, the coma might be irreversible. And this was certainly not what I went into the church for. So I had to husband my emotional and energy resources carefully.

My ordeal went on for at least five hours. Then suddenly, while standing behind the door, dejected and on the brink of despair, the door opened, and standing in front of me were two fresh-looking young Americans. They were both tall and looked in the pink of health. They shouted almost in unison, "What are you doing here? How did you get here?"

I shouted back, "Please, get me out! I want to get out now! Now!" But they kept repeating, "How did you get in?"

Tempers were rising high, so I said, "Gentlemen, let's sit down and talk." So all three of us sat down; and I, sweating and panting a bit, said, "Look, I am not a thief or a burglar. As you can see for yourself, the place has not been broken into. All that happened was that I saw your door wide open about five hours ago when I came in. I meditated, looked around, and prayed, that's all. I must then have fallen asleep, for earlier I had heard two male voices from where the pipe organ is. And when I got up and walked to the door, I found it locked. Since then I have been banging at it intermittently, hoping that the police or someone would come in to let me out. Gentlemen, that's all, that's the end of my story." I paused briefly, and then added, "Look, to assure you, let me tell you that a few years ago, I visited your main church in Salt Lake City and was shown around by one of your elders."

Their faces lit up with broad friendly smiles. We then shook hands firmly and hugged each other. Now it was my turn to be the interrogator. With my credentials established as a genuine worshipper and not a thief, and a rapport robustly established between us, I asked them, "Gentlemen, may I now ask you just a couple of questions following your long and grueling grilling of me?"

"Sure," said the older of the two. He appeared to be senior in rank to his colleague.

"Are you ready for my inquisition?" I asked them; they both replied in the affirmative. So I shot off, "What on earth made you come here now?"

"That's a good question," replied the gentleman, by the name of Peter. "Well, at about seven, Tom called me and said that he felt that we must come to the church. As we were not scheduled to be here till tomorrow afternoon, I did not see much merit in his request. We discussed it briefly on the phone, and that was the end of the conversation. Ten or so minutes later, he called me again and repeated that there was an inner still voice persistently telling him, loud and clear, that we must come to the church.

"But I still felt that it would not be the best use of our time to come here now and again tomorrow afternoon. But he was so persistent and persuasive, and he would not budge. Neither did I. Again, our conversation ended as before."

Tom smiled approvingly but said nothing. His friend continued, "When Brother Tom called again the third time with the same request, I had become so weary of his persistence and determined doggedness that I asked him to come along pronto as he had kept repeating that the call to go to the church was urgent, very urgent.

"So he came along to my apartment, and we drove here, wondering all along what was in store for us here."

Tom then interjected, "We opened the door, and lo and behold, standing behind the door was you. We were completely taken aback. Just could not believe our eyes, for we were 100 percent sure that there was no one, not a single soul in the church, when we locked it. So you can now understand our puzzlement and consternation when we saw you."

Peter then said, "This indeed was divine intervention, nothing else." He paused, then reflecting said, "What made Brother Tom call me so persistently, almost to the point of annoying me?" For a brief moment, there was complete silence. Then we held our hands together and prayed to God for his divine and mighty wonders and works. The prayer was led by Peter.

With the mission to the church accomplished, they drove me in their car to the railway station, where I took the last train to town where the hotel was.

By the time I reached the hotel, Breid had been fretting for hours, fearing that I had perhaps been kidnapped or been beaten up by some racist youths or had been involved in an accident, for I was eight hours behind schedule. Rather disheveled and dejected, but at the same time elated with the outcome of my ordeal, I was ecstatic as I told Breid and our two Dutch friends about my ordeal and how in the end it was not the police but rather two young American Mormon missionaries that got me out of my predicament.

It was such a joy seeing my wife again, for at the crisis point in my plight, I did wonder whether we would meet again.

Tropical Down Pour

It was a Saturday, and the afternoon was unusually hot even for a tropical country. Although the sky appeared covered with thick clouds, signifying rain, my wife and I were determined to attend a political rally in Accra. It was billed as the last and most important of the election campaign rallies. And we were determined to be there as part of history.

Being sticklers for time, we were at the venue an hour before the scheduled time. When we reached the spot, it was crowded with thousands standing in the open field. We stopped our car a good distance from the platform meant for the invited guests. Normally, Breid would be the first to walk to her seat. But on this occasion, she adamantly refused to leave the car. I pleaded with her again and again, but she refused to budge. So in utter frustration, I decided to go alone, and I asked our driver to stay with the car until I return. I carefully noted the spot where the car was parked.

Gingerly, I made my way to the platform with about seventy seats on it and sat down. Although the roof was plastic, it could withstand the searing heat against which it was built. The wooden floor was solid and firm but could break up if the persons sitting or standing on it increased beyond the expected number.

Suddenly, without any warning whatsoever, it began to rain mightily, accompanied by thunder and lightning. The rain gathered momentum, and in a matter of a few minutes, had turned into a tropical down pour. Raining cats and dogs in the temperate zones paled into insignificance compared with this unleashing of its tropical equivalent.

The crowd grew bigger and bigger with the rain and storm. To liven up the scene, loudspeakers blasted famous, well-known patriotic and national songs into the air. The people, undeterred by the fury of the elements, stood their ground, dancing and singing.

Those of us who were already seated had little choice but to bear the heavy drops of rain falling on our heads and shoulders. Grumbling or complaining was out of the question as we watched the enthusiasm and exuberance of the crowd before us heavily drenched

Sadly, the special guest speakers and keynote speakers for the event did not show up for the next couple of hours when the rain had stopped and the sky was dry and clear. Then they came in a convoy of cars blaring sirens, escorted by police outriders and led by a police vehicle.

Despite what they had gone through, the people listened patiently to all the speeches. Their theme was the same—to continue the good and noble work of the previous administration if voted into power and provide more jobs, clean water, education, roads, housing, and hospitals. Although the people were used to hearing these and similar promises throughout the election campaign, they loudly shouted and clapped approvingly as speaker after speaker went on.

As it was getting darker and the skies more ominous again, the grand occasion was brought to a happy end. The special guests then were driven furiously away, similar to their arrival and in a manner that could endanger their own lives and those who had borne enormous stress and inconvenience to wait and hear them.

The crowd, estimated to be over fifty thousand, began to disperse. Despite the few electric bulbs hoisted over the grounds, the whole place was pitch dark Finding my way out had thus become a major challenge. To compound my problems, my mobile phone had been inactivated by the rain and lightning. In any case, Breid had not brought hers with her.

So gingerly, I tried to make my way through the thick mud and droplets of rain to the spot where I knew that Breid would be waiting for me. I turned left toward the car but was firmly stopped by a tall policeman. He was manning a makeshift exit. In spite of all my pleas and requests, he simply refused to let me through. Naturally, I was angry and upset. I felt that he must be one of the public servants who was clothed with a bit of power and authority and delighted in exercising it to the fullest.

Rather upset and put out, I decided to try my luck at another exit after I had walked a few yards straight ahead of me. Again, it was the same story of a robust rebuff, with the policeman stretching his hands wide to let me know that in no uncertain terms, he would not give way to me. I had some difficulty preventing myself from telling him my piece of mind, but I succeeded and kept a tight control on my mouth.

The rain was beginning to wear me down, but it was still bearable. For being tropical rain, it was rather warm; and from my elementary school days, I had become used to wading through to go to school.

Being a firm believer in the old saying "If you first try and do not succeed, try, try, and try again" and its ancillary adage "Third time lucky," I made a final and third effort to extricate myself from my predicament. My shoes were soaked and dirty, but my spirits were not down although not as high as they should be.

The third encounter resulted in no joy, except that this time, the burly officer on duty was rather unpleasant. I was forced to say, "Look, Officer, all that I am trying to do is to find the shortest route to where my car is parked with my wife in it, and you are not being in any way helpful."

He shrugged his shoulders, smiled, and said, "Big man, I am only doing my duty. You cannot pass here, sorry."

My further pleas got me nowhere. And in utter frustration, I burst out, "Some of you officers are very inconsiderate. The little power and authority that is bestowed on you is exercised rather capriciously to the bane of the public who pay you. I know that you are in charge here, but to my knowledge, you are not yet in charge of the country. The elections after this rally will decide, thank you."

I heard him shout, "You foolish big man! You cannot talk to me like that. Who do you think you are, the president?"

With that, wet as I was, I turned right and started to walk toward the street, in the direction away from where the car was parked. It took me another twenty minutes of almost blind maneuvering in the dark through the people still there. I was angry with myself and wondered what had happened to Breid. My aim was to reach the street, then walk leftward toward the car or call a taxicab if she was not there.

My head was bowed down all the time that I walked. Just as I approached a huge open gutter on the side of the street, I raised my head and was about to shout "taxi" or walk leftward as planned, when to my complete amazement and shock I saw Breid at the back of the car with the door wide open. She had a broad and warm smile and, stretching her hands toward me, shouted, "Joseph!" I was flabbergasted and nearly dropped on the street.

"Where on earth have you been, dear? I have been worrying about you all the time. What happened?"

I responded with, "And what happened to you? How did you end here, darling? Just unbelievable."

I sat with her, and her story began to unfold. "Just after you left, a hefty policeman came and ordered me to move, saying that where I had stopped was only for VIPs. I tried to reason with him, but he was adamant. Would not budge at all. Just as you did when we arrived, you remember?" I interjected.

She continued, "No sooner had I settled at this spot than another police officer—this time, a woman—came to order me to move. For according to her, where I was parked was interfering with traffic. I tried to persuade her to let me stay, but she was insistent. Then after about thirty minutes of arguing and pleading, she was suddenly friendly and said, 'You can stay, but don't do it again.'

"I thanked her warmly, and she left. So although one or two passersby banged at the side of the car and shouted '*Obroni*! (white person),' I did not budge or move from here but kept praying for you. So relieved and nice to see you again, thank God! And that ends my story, darling.

"And what is yours, dear?"

"Well, it is a long story that, to me, demonstrates divine intervention in the affairs of men, certainly in my life." She listened with incredulity to my story of my failed attempts to go to the spot where she was originally parked and had been moved by police power.

We hugged and kissed each other, and I said, "Indeed, God moves in mysterious ways. Who said there is no God?" And with that, we asked our driver to take us home.

Index

A

Accra, 14, 18, 26, 32, 35, 39, 46, 50, 54, 62
Achimota, 9–10, 12, 41, 43
Africa, 10–12, 25, 33, 58–59
Agona Swedru, 10, 14, 17, 40, 45
Amamoo, Joseph Godson
   daughters of, 49, 53, 56
   as editor, 17, 34–38, 42
   on failure, 9–10, 14, 16, 19
   father of, 10, 13, 15–16, 33
   illness of, 32
      medical ambition of, 13, 16, 19, 23, 26–29, 32, 42–43, 50
   mother of, 9–12, 15, 17, 36, 41, 43
   in prison, 29, 33–34, 37, 47, 54–56
   victory of, 18
ambassador, 17–18, 32–34, 37, 54
applications, 16
appointments, 18, 37, 42
assets, 29, 33–34, 38, 41, 50
Austria, 29, 31

B

bank accounts, 29, 38, 47
Batten, John, 32
biology, 13, 20
Breid, 7, 31, 33–35, 37–39, 49–53, 56–57, 61–64
Britain, 10, 13, 15–16, 26–29, 41, 43

C

campaign, 18–19, 26
Cape Coast, 9, 15, 45
Castle (Ghana's White House), 19, 34, 36
chief administrator, 23–25
chief director, 27
chief of staff, 27, 46, 51–52
church, 11, 52, 59, 61
civil servants, 20, 33, 41–43, 46, 52
college, 11–12
coma, 59
congress, 17–18
conscience, 31–32, 51

conviction, 15, 21, 27, 42–43
corruption, 21, 45
coup, 34, 37–38, 56

D

dean, 27, 29
deputy minister, 18, 43, 47, 50
diamonds, 43–44, 50, 58
diplomat, 17, 34–35
doctors
  foreign, 26–27, 50
  supervisor of, 23, 29
duty, moral, 35–36

E

editorials, 38–39
education, 9, 12, 18, 26, 41, 43, 63
Edward, 35–36
elections, 17–18, 64
examinations, 9–11, 13–14, 28, 32

F

file, 20–22, 46, 55
Fred, 9–10

G

Germany, 24–25
Ghana, 11, 14–15, 17–19, 25–26, 29, 31–37, 41, 43–45, 47–48, 52, 58
Ghanaian Times, 17, 34, 36
gold, 29, 43–44, 50, 58
government, 18–19, 27, 33, 36, 49, 54
government ministers, 24, 33, 42–43, 51–52, 54

H

hardship, 9, 20, 26, 29, 32
health ministry, 19, 21, 23, 26–27, 43, 50
hospitals, 12, 19, 23–25, 32, 43, 50, 63
hotel, 36–37, 59, 61
housing problem, 50, 56
Hungary, 26, 29, 35–36

I

incidents, 19, 26, 31, 58–59
interview, 10, 14, 16, 36–37
Israel, 34, 56–57

J

John, 49–57
Juju men, 11, 15
junta, 37–38

K

karma, 40
knowledge, 16–17, 32, 35

L

Lands and Mineral Resources, 43, 50–51
letter, 11, 14, 22, 32, 45–47, 55
Lisbon, 58–59
London, 11, 15–18, 32, 34–37, 39
LPC (last pay certificate), 20

M

medical schools, 15–16, 27
medicine, 11, 16–17, 26, 28
military coup, 26, 33–34, 36, 39, 47, 55

military junta, 29, 35–36, 38
Ministry of Health office (Accra), 27
misfortune, 15, 31, 33, 37
Moscow, 49
Mr. Prah, 52

N

Natasia, 56–57
Nkrumah, 17–18, 26, 31

P

party, center-right, 17
party leader, 18
Peter, 47, 60–61
political prisoners, 55–56
Portugal, 58–59
power, 11, 37, 45, 48, 50, 63–64
president, 26, 31, 33
prison officer, senior, 49

R

religions, 40
Russia, 26–27

S

scholarships, 10–11, 26
schools, 9–11, 13, 27, 46, 63
science subjects, 13–14
surgeons, 28–29, 43

T

Tarkwa, 20
Tom, 60–61
Transatlantic Slave Trade, 58

U

United States of America, 17, 24–25

V

VIPs, 51–52, 64

W

West Africa, 32, 35, 41